T0318192

The Way Forward

The Way Forward

Lean Leadership and Systems Thinking for
Large and Small Businesses

Wallace Garneau

Routledge
Taylor & Francis Group

A PRODUCTIVITY PRESS BOOK

First Edition published 2021
by Routledge
600 Broken Sound Parkway #300, Boca Raton FL, 33487

and by Routledge
2 Park Square, Milton Park, Abingdon, Oxon, OX14 4RN

Routledge is an imprint of the Taylor & Francis Group, an informa business

© 2021 Wallace Garneau

Library of Congress Cataloging-in-Publication Data
A catalog record for this title has been requested

ISBN: 978-0-367-76200-1 (hbk)
ISBN: 978-0-367-56539-8 (pbk)
ISBN: 978-1-003-16591-0 (ebk)

Typeset in Minion Pro
by Spi Global, India

Contents

Acknowledgments

I have many people I would like to acknowledge, both for the knowledge that went into this book and for the inspiration to write it. First, I want to thank my wife, without whose love and dedication I would never have undertaken this project. I love you, Gosia! I want to thank all of the professors under whom I have studied over the years, and particularly Doctor Mark Perry, who, though we did not get along when I took his economics class, instilled in me a love of economics that has continued, and which is sprinkled throughout this work. (He also runs a brilliant blog called Carpe Diem.) I want to thank the people who made the MBA Oath, whose ideals all business people should strive to fulfill. I want to thank W. Edwards Deming, whose ideas have been an inspiration to me, and Taiichi Ohno, who put Deming's ideas into practice. I want to thank my mother, Joan Garneau, for editing this book, and for the upbringing that, along with my father, Ted Garneau, has been instrumental in everything I have ever done. I thank Mike McCarthy, author of *Sustain Your Gains*, for his technical editing. I want to thank all of my employers, both past and present (including my first employer – McDonalds), for all the experience I have acquired along the way. I want to give a special shout-out to our military services, and particularly the two I served in: the Marine Corps and the Army. Semper Fi, Devil Dogs!

I would like to thank Magda Tabaszewski for producing the artwork and figures for this book.

Last but not least, I want to thank my fellow travelers, Ed Potoczak and Greg Tripple, whose friendship and business acumen contributed deeply to my own.

About the Author

Wallace Garneau is a two-service military veteran, with four years in the United States Marine Corps Reserve and four years in the United States Army. He has twenty-four years of experience in process improvement roles, having served as the E-Commerce Manager, the IT Manager, and/or the Director of Business Systems for various medium and large manufacturing companies, and currently works for one of the world's largest technology companies. Wallace holds a Bachelor's of Science degree in Information Technologies and Telecommunications from the University of Phoenix, and an MBA degree in Lean Manufacturing from the University of Michigan. He is currently finishing a Master's of Science in Lean Manufacturing from Kettering University.

Wallace is a published poet and essayist, with articles in *Information World* and *Computer World*. Wallace runs the popular blog, The Daily Libertarian (thedailylibertarian.com) and is nationally syndicated on Global Liberty Media (globallibertymedia.com).

In this, Wallace's first book, he examines the political and economic shortcomings of the United States today, how these shortcomings can negatively impact businesses operations, and what business owners, managers, and employees can do to better focus on the value they add, making their organizations faster, leaner, and more competitive. If you want to learn how to create more value for your customers, at less cost than your competitors, within the friendly realm of free-market capitalism, this is the book for you.

Introduction
(A Personal Odyssey)

The inspiration to write this book came from, of all things, a job.

Years ago, while studying for my MBA, I met a career coach named Alan, and through Alan, met a guy named Bill. The three of us became friends.

Several years later, Alan, Bill, and I went to a gun show in Novi, Michigan. It was about an hour's drive, so we rode together. On the way there, Alan told us a fascinating story about an induction heating company that had gotten about as big as it could with the founder running it by himself. The owner, Alan told us, was a great engineer, but not a business person, making this company the proverbial "diamond in the rough" we might be able to grow into an induction heating powerhouse.

A couple of years later, the owner of this company contracted Alan to bring in new talent (Alan was eventually hired in as a full-time employee). Alan brought with him a high-powered CFO named Robert, and began recruiting Bill to work as General Manager. Even before Bill was hired, Alan and Bill began talking about bringing me in as the final piece of the Executive Team.

Bill and Alan did not feel that this company had the information systems it needed. It was, in fact, sorely lacking in IT, though it did have a decent IT Manager. There were also several really important parts of the company, like Service and Repair, that were poorly managed. Finally, this company was a very small player in the induction heating world. Bill and Alan thought my lean manufacturing background could help to improve operations.

Within a week of Bill coming on board, Alan asked him, "Is it time to bring in Wally?" Bill said yes.

I like nothing better than taking part in truly competitive industries, and outperforming competitors until they have no chance to catch-up. *That* is what I set out to help this company do, and it is also what this book is about: building a business that creates value so thoroughly and so efficiently, that competing directly against it is not feasible. Getting the kind of performance needed from this company would require changes in how the company did things, which in turn would require a very different culture from that already in place.

The first rule of cultural change is to wait at least two weeks before changing anything, both to give employees an appearance of continuity, and also to find out why things are done the way they currently are. The second rule is not to change too much too fast, even after the two weeks are up. It is important that as a new leader starts to make changes, the first few are wins.

Most people are resistant to change, and as a result, most companies that go through true cultural transformations lose around a third of their personnel. The most important factor in determining the success or failure of such a transformation is the executive team, which must be willing to let a third of the workforce go, including some of those the company may want to keep. If the executive team is unified behind the changes, then radical cultural change is possible, but if the upper executives are not united in favor of the new culture, then change will fail.

These were the kinds of changes I was hired to make.

The interview process was interesting. Bill and I (and sometimes Alan) were having strategy sessions a month before I was even recruited. By the time I began to interview, some of my ideas were already starting to be implemented, making my hiring somewhat of a foregone conclusion.

When I met the owner, I found him to be friendly (though somewhat distant), and extremely knowledgeable about induction heating. He did not ask many questions, but talked a lot about his company. It seemed far more important to him that I understood *his* value, and that of his *company*, than that he understand how I could add value. In retrospect, that made some sense, given that he was hiring me on the advice of others.

The company was living hand to mouth. When payroll went out, it was often unclear whether there would be enough money in the bank to cover the checks. The owner would send the checks out anyway, hoping that money from a customer would arrive before employees cashed their checks, often with a statement like, "Well, I've been lucky before."

When I accepted the job, the lack of financial stability gave me a moment of pause, but I had never failed at any job in my life, and as I toured the facility, I could clearly see both waste and opportunities to improve operations. With absolute faith in Alan, Robert, Bill, and myself, I took the job.

I should have paid closer attention to the owner's readiness to change.

The company had been profitable before, and the owner believed that if the company could only get back to doing things the exact same way it had done things before, profits would return. In the owner's estimation, what the company lacked was control, and if he could just clone himself 75 times, all of his problems would go away.

In reality, the products the company produced were very different than what it produced when it was profitable. The company was founded on a very specific innovation in power supplies, and when the company was new, all it made were those power supplies. Eventually, other companies improved their power supplies, and this company needed to start making full induction heating machines to remain competitive.

It became clear very quickly that Bill had been hired to be a babysitter more than a general manager, and he was taken to task by the owner whenever he showed the least initiative. His job was to control employees rather than to improve operations. Alan was left planning expansions and building improvements without the money to fund them, and he was berated whenever he did spend money, even if he'd been given permission to do so. Robert, being in charge of the finances of a sinking ship, had no opportunity to see eye to eye with an owner who believed that his employees, rather than his operations, were the cause of his problems. The owner did not listen to any of us.

For about six months, we Four Horsemen fought tooth and nail to improve operations. Some improvements stuck, and others did not. Alan had a very short term viewpoint. He was always telling the rest of us that "we are on a burning platform," and when we would look for root-causes of the "burning platforms," he would tell us that "we have to live to get there" and that our insights and ideas would take too long to come to fruition. In Alan's eyes, we had to go through a hiring and firing process, getting rid of bad employees, reducing headcount, and hiring more top-tier talent, to pull the company away from the abyss. In other words, we had to do exactly what Alan thought every company had to do, whenever times were tough (Figure I.1).

To be fair to Alan, he knew the owner better than did the rest of us and had an idea what the owner would and would not let us do. I think Alan understood that our hands were tied and was trying to steer us toward doing what we could within our constraints, even if those actions would be counter-productive. The rest of us were acting as if we had somewhat of a free hand to improve company operations when we did not.

In my estimation, the real issue was not a lack of talent, but disconnects between different parts of the company. Bill and Robert agreed 100% (and though Alan did not agree 100%, he did not disagree, either). The sales process, for example, was nonexistent, and the sales team made too many

FIGURE I.1
The Burning Platform

assumptions about what the customer "really needed" (as opposed to what customers said they needed), and as a result, engineering would design machines that did not meet customer expectations. There were other problems, but these were the biggest.

Induction heating is not a very complicated process. It involves sending a lot of electricity into copper coils to create a varying-magnetic field. When a conducting material (like metal) is placed into the coils, resistance to the varying-magnetic field heats it up. An induction heating machine can heat metal to a given temperature in seconds, which is useful for forging, heat-treating, and various other things.

The hard part of induction heating is the level of control needed to get a piece of metal to an exact temperature. The copper coils heat up when a piece of metal is passed through them, so the coils have to be kept cool (the coils are hollow, and water is run through them). The *number* of coils used is a critical factor as well – each coil is expensive, but if there are not enough coils, the coils will burn-up. Induction heating also involves some level of danger, mixing massive amounts of electricity with high levels of running water.

The company was pretty good at the actual induction process (other than often trying to use too few coils to save money), but each machine was a custom build with very specific material-handling requirements, and we struggled with the material handling.

The owner was largely absent. He was the only member of the sales team who actually closed anything, and, as such, whenever we were broke, he traveled. There was a pattern to this: we'd run broke and the owner would travel to sell things, then we'd have enough business to get our heads above water, and the owner would come home. Shortly thereafter, we'd go broke again and the owner would travel.

Another major problem was that any profit made on current jobs largely went to fund repair work on previous jobs. We charged customers for repair work when we could, but most of the repair work covered design flaws, and we could not charge the customer for mistakes that were our fault.

xviii • *Introduction (A Personal Odyssey)*

When the owner was home, he'd stroll in at 4:00 or 4:30 PM (shortly after all the workers on the plant went home), and start tearing apart whatever was being built. To a degree this was justified, given that the owner/sales person had not previously shared with the engineers all of the customer requirements. The owner would see that what was being completed on the plant floor was not what the customer asked for, so the owner would have it torn down and built again, with costly changes.

Robert, as the CFO of an essentially bankrupt company, was under the most stress, and had the sharpest disagreements with the owner. He was fired after about six months.

I lasted a year, and then I was asked to leave.

Bill was asked to leave shortly after I was. Alan lasted another six months. As of my writing this, the company is about 75% smaller then it was when we left, and is still struggling along, on the edge of bankruptcy.

The lessons in this book were learned from the failure of that induction heating company.

I do not believe that my former employer is alone in the world. I think similar struggles exist in organizations of all sizes. As such, I believe a book like this one could be an invaluable resource to a great many companies, big and small alike. Failure is a powerful teacher.

Organizations that do not standardize operations use too much time and energy to produce their products and services, resulting in higher prices to customers. Consider driving to work as an example. I follow the same route every day, giving me a standard route. Imagine if I had to take a different route to work every day – how much time and energy would I have to waste trying to figure out how to find a new route every day rather than just using the same one each time? How much variance would I be adding to the time it took me to get to work by changing routes every day?

The purpose of this book is to blend modern management theories with the culture of lean (and perhaps a sprinkling of economics) to show today's business leaders how to create organizations that are as customer-oriented and as efficient in delivering value as possible. If one thinks of each role in an organization as a spot on an assembly line, where everything each person does creates output someone else uses, the question becomes whether or not each person's activities maximize the effectiveness of others. Do we, as organizations, set ourselves up for success, or for failure? Most companies, if they answer honestly, would say, "A little bit of both." This book is about helping those companies improve.

Business owners will no doubt find value in reading *The Way Forward: Lean Leadership and Systems Thinking for Large and Small Businesses,* but so too will lower level managers who aspire to become top-level managers, and even entry-level workers who want to know how best to help their employers succeed. I wrote this with a hope of changing the culture of American business to make us more competitive, globally.

The word, "competitive," is counter-intuitive in America, as it makes us look at other companies either as customers for whose business we compete or as companies we compete against. We often lose sight of the fact that to be more competitive, we must also be better at collaborating. Apple, for example, allows third-party developers to sell apps for the iPhone. The variety of apps makes the iPhone a better product than it would otherwise be. Companies do not just become "competitive" by building cheaper products with fewer defects than do others, but by building products that *better integrate into the world around us* than do others. We compete by providing more *value* than anyone else.

Note: People tend to hear the term "lean," and immediately they think of manufacturing. That's a mistake. Lean concepts are applicable everywhere, and as you get into this book, you'll begin to see how you can apply these concepts in your environment, whatever that environment might be.

Readers of this book can expect to learn:

- How to Drive Business through Adding Value
- How to Scale Up – and Back Down (if necessary)
- How to Handle Downturns Without Layoffs
- When, Where, How, and Why to Automate
- How to Handle Maturing Markets (and How to Disrupt New Ones)
- How and Why to Implement One Piece Flow

- How and Why to Implement Rapid Change Over
- The Importance of Statistics-Based Management (and How to Implement)
- How and Why to Standardize Operations
- A Better Way to Look at Quality
- How to Build a Better Supply Chain
- How to Use Employees AS Resources
- PERT-Based Project Management
- To Rethink Strategic Decision-Making
- To Align Marketing and Engineering

1

The Corrupt Way to Make Money

Before getting into the concept of Lean Leadership, I want to go into a brief political and economic discussion about the state of business in America today, for the techniques in this book are based on free-market dynamics that are much weaker than they were in the past. This book assumes that the way for a business to make money is to find a need that customers are willing to pay to have met, and then to meet that need better than other companies. This book assumes, for example, that if air bags sell in cars, it is because the public is willing to pay more for cars with air bags, and not because the government mandated that cars have air bags. This book assumes that if wind turbines and solar panels sell, it is because they provide energy more cost effectively than do alternative sources, and not because the government decided we should have more solar panels and wind turbines.

This book assumes things that are, over time, becoming less true.

That's not to say that the techniques in this book do not work, because they do. We still have free-market elements to our economy, and as long as we do, the methods in this book will be effective. This book would, however, be incomplete if I did not recognize that in our current, cronyist system, there are other ways a company can make money, rather than by pleasing customers. This chapter looks at how to use cronyism to make money, which stands in stark contrast to the rest of the book. I do not endorse cronyism, but it is important for the public to understand what a "mixed economy" really looks like, in the hope of one day restoring our free-market system, such that someday adding value can be the *only* way to make money.

There is a book called *Executive Greed*,[1] by Vinay B. Kothari, which I read as a part of a business ethics class. *Executive Greed* discusses how corrupt the US Economy currently is. *Executive Greed* doesn't say how to make money in a gamed system, but it does discuss just how gamed the system is – and it is truly a system in which "we the people" are exploited, for the benefit of the economic elite.

I also studied nonmarket strategies in my MBA program, and I will never forget the studies we made on the pharmaceutical industry, which provides a great example on just how bad things have become.

DECEPTIVE ADVERTISING

It was not that long ago that pharmaceutical companies were not allowed to market directly to consumers. Pharmaceuticals are, by nature, prescribed by doctors, and it was thought that while consumers might be the ones who consume pharmaceuticals, doctors really are the ones best positioned to determine when to use them. The pharmaceutical industry lobbied government long and hard to have the rules changed, and today it is perfectly legal for pharmaceutical companies to advertise directly to consumers.

At first, pharmaceutical companies had to follow truth in advertising laws that said that their advertisements had to be true, and, in fact, some advertisements were taken off the air for making claims that could not be supported, such as a toe fungus commercial, in which a giant pill rolls over a fungus monster. The pill was not effective, so having a pill kill the monster was deemed by the FDA as being in violation of truth in advertising laws.

In time, pharmaceutical companies were able to lobby government, to allow pharmaceutical advertisements to say anything that was not demonstrably false.

That sounds like a small change, but think of the implications. If a pharmaceutical company markets a pill "for" a particular ailment, and the pharmaceutical company has to follow truth in advertising laws, then that pill had better work, for saying it "is taken for" an ailment implies that it has a positive effect. Change the law so that pharmaceutical companies can say anything that is not expressly false, and suddenly, as long as they can *get* people to take a pill "for" a particular ailment, they can advertise the pill as "taken *for*" an ailment, even if it does not work. Under this interpretation, pharmaceutical companies could sell pills "for" ailments for which the pills did absolutely nothing. Suddenly, the airwaves became bombarded with advertisements for pills, "taken for" different ailments, with no regard for how effective those pills may actually be. The most common advertisements are for pills "taken to enhance that special part of the male anatomy." As I write this, none of the pills currently on the market taken to enhance that special part of the male anatomy, have any positive impact on any part of the male anatomy.

Not to stop there, the pharmaceutical companies began to pay doctors to tour the country, giving presentations on "new" ailments that did not previously exist, which the pharmaceutical companies could sell their medications as being "taken for." These are "ailments" pharmaceutical companies made up out of thin air, and pharmaceutical companies, at the time we studied them, made more than half their revenue selling medications that did not work, treating ailments that did not exist.

Pharmaceutical companies are also protected from litigation when their products harm consumers. As long as they run really small print, telling those who see their advertisements all of the innumerable ways their products might hurt people, they are protected from anyone suing them.

The interesting thing about this pharmaceutical example is that on first glance, it sounds like the government needs to correct for the free market, but the root cause of all the problems is that the government has protected pharmaceutical companies from the harm their products may do to consumers. Everything else the government has done has been in response to problems caused by this violation of free-market standards – standards in which the courts are the proper mechanism to address harm.

There are only three kinds of politicians: those who can be persuaded, those who can be intimidated, and those who can be bought.

A.P. GIANNINI, FOUNDER, BANK OF AMERICA, quoted in *The Innovation Stack*, by Jim McKelvey[2]

FORCED TO BUY A PRODUCT

Ethanol is another great example. Corn farmers have convinced the government to mandate that ethanol be added to gasoline. Ethanol is made from corn, and burns both hotter, and faster, than does gasoline. The ethanol mandates make both corn and gasoline more expensive, while making cars less fuel-efficient. Ethanol mandates hurt everyone except the corn farmer.

The lesson is that in today's economy, companies can enhance their ability to make money by lobbying government, rather than by making goods and services that benefit customers. Because lobbying activities are not considered "competitive," companies can even collude in such activities as "industry groups." Sadly, getting government to intervene in markets can, in certain circumstances, be more effective than producing goods and services people actually want (like gasoline without ethanol).

Making goods and services which meet legitimate customer needs better than competitors is a very dog-eat-dog world. This is a consumer-friendly environment rather than a business-friendly environment. Socialists often claim that free markets favor corporations, but that is not true. Free markets favor consumers and are unforgiving on businesses, of any size, that do not meet the needs of consumers. In a free market, if a small competitor can better meet the needs of consumers than can a giant corporation, the small competitor will grow and the giant corporation will shrink. Given time, the giant corporation may become a small competitor and may go completely out of business, whereas what was a small competitor can become a giant corporation. Apple started in a garage, but look at it today. It is only when markets are not free that corporations can use regulatory barriers to squash smaller competitors, and to maintain their positions, independently of how well they serve customers.

CUSTOMER NEEDS OR POLITICAL NEEDS?

Companies can find products that meet *political* needs (chosen by politicians rather than expressed by customers, that is, such as regulations on air and water, consumer safety, reducing $co2$ emissions, etc.). The type of political need does not matter as long as there is one. It does not have to be a *legitimate* political need either, and the "solution" need not be effective. As long as the cause is considered "noble," even a bad solution will get good press, and government support.

When dealing with political needs, it is actually better if goods and services have as little effect as possible, such that the "need" for those goods and services does not go away. This dynamic also creates job security for politicians.

One company I worked for made money through government grants, by spraying coal with fire hoses. "Clean Coal" was a popular political goal at the time. Spraying coal with water had no effect on the coal (other than making it wet), but it earned this company tens of millions of dollars a year in federal grants, and was the principal way a big part of this company (not the part I worked for) earned revenue. This company operation was dishonest, but it satisfied a political goal.

Once a company has goods and services that meet political needs, it can then figure out how to get the government to help. Government can create tax breaks for those who buy the company's products (think Tesla), government can create subsidies to offset the company's expenses, government can make regulations requiring that a company's products be included as "safety devices" on bigger products (like cars), or government can purchase a company's goods and services directly.

Companies can take out government loans. CEOs and other executives can pay themselves handsomely, with high salaries and bonuses, while doing almost nothing, and then push the company into bankruptcy once the loans dry up. Solyndra did this, and it is a perfectly legal Ponzi-like scheme. Once Solyndra went out of business, there was nothing stopping the people who built Solyndra from taking out more government loans, to start more companies, meeting more political needs (instead of the real needs of real consumers). Ponzi-like schemes based on government loans are a great way to make lots of money in a relatively short period of time, all at the taxpayer's expense.

What Solyndra did was similar to a Ponzi-scheme, but sometimes the government assists companies in creating actual Ponzi-schemes. According to court documents, between 2011 and 2018, an Obama-era company called D. C. Solar manufactured mobile solar generator units, on trailers, to provide temporary power during power outages, for sporting events, cell towers, etc.

Federal tax credits made the company seem like a sound investment, but according to the DOJ, "The conspirators pulled off their scheme by selling solar generators that did not exist to investors, making it appear that solar generators existed in locations that they did not, creating false financial statements, and obtaining false lease contracts, among other efforts to conceal the fraud." The DOJ labeled D. C. Solar as a billion-dollar Ponzi scheme.

ACTUAL RESULTS OR VIRTUE SIGNALING?

With enough capital, someone can even try to organize the public to create a brand new political need, and then be the first company in a position to make money on it. Al Gore did this with Global Warming, and should we ever put in place a cap-and-trade, carbon credit system, Al Gore, who has positioned himself as the owner of the company that will manage the carbon credits, will immediately become a billionaire – without reducing actual carbon consumption.

George Soros provides another great example. There was no statistical evidence to support the contention that our police forces try to harm the public, or that the police specifically target African Americans, but George Soros (and others) spent hundreds of millions of dollars making the public believe these things to be true, and as a result, companies which make body cameras (which police are increasingly being forced to wear), and other things designed to monitor police conduct, stand to make a tremendous amount of money, by having it mandated that police use these things.

The policing of police is rapidly becoming a major new industry, and the fact that the police no longer want to do their jobs, out of fear of being the next YouTube sensation, has been a bonanza for security companies.

Security is a real need, but even where a company provides a legitimate need, government can still help grow profitability. If I ran a company that had more secure doors and windows than anyone else, it might make sense for me to push government to mandate that my products be included in all new housing construction. I probably could not make government mandate that *my* products *specifically* be used, but I might be able to have regulations crafted that create barriers to entry for anyone else who wants to enter my market sphere, giving me a leg up on any potential competitors.

Once a company has created, or identified, political needs, has created goods or services to service those political needs, and has identified all of the things they would like government to do, all that is left is to lobby government. Companies can lobby Congress to have new laws created. More likely, companies can lobby bureaucrats in different regulatory bodies already in existence, to utilize laws already on the books, in ways that direct tax dollars into their company, and keep competitors out.

MORE GOVERNMENT = LESS BENEFIT TO CONSUMERS

Keep in mind too that the more government gets involved in the use of goods and services, the less it matters whether or not those goods and services provide any benefit. The object here is not to benefit society, but to fleece it. The object is not to circumvent unnecessary red tape in order to bring products to market, but to make red tape the source of one's profit, and to push for more red tape to protect profit. The more choice the consumer has, the more benefit the consumer will demand before they purchase products. If the public has no choice, then whether or not any actual benefit is provided by the goods and services produced is irrelevant.

Consider the CFL lightbulb. Congress mandated that incandescent lightbulbs be phased-out, and pushed for the implementation of CFL lightbulbs, even though CFL lightbulbs did not last longer than incandescent lightbulbs, and contained dangerous levels of mercury. CFL lightbulbs cost more than incandescent lightbulbs, so pushing their usage was great for the companies that made these bulbs, but it was not good for the consumer. Had it not been for the free-market introduction of LED lightbulbs, we might have been in real trouble!

Another approach is to lobby government to grandfather a company out of legal requirements new companies will have to meet, such as allowing existing power plants to operate without meeting emissions restrictions. New power plants built by competitors would, of course, have to meet the expensive restrictions.

Try to find things one does that are expensive to copy, and that competitors do not do. Even if a company cannot force competitors out of business, through regulatory oversight, they may be able to have regulations written and/or used in ways that discourage new entrants from entering the market. Whatever the case, government can protect businesses from competition, and without competition (or with less competition), it is easier to make money than it is in a free and open market; with less supply, prices are higher for customers.

Increasingly in today's economy, consumers are not a source of business profit, other than through the taxes they pay. Consumers can CHOOSE whether or not to buy goods and services in a free market, whereas, if a company has government create their demand, the government can pump tax money directly into that company, can mandate that consumers buy that company's products, and can use subsidies and regulatory authority to boost the company's profitability. The more a company can remove consumer choice from their operations, the less the will of the public will threaten continued operations. As long as a company continues to grease the wheels of the bureaucratic system, it will do well. Government bureaucracy replaces the consumer as the end-customer.

Why things work this way is relatively simple: the public has a short attention span. Something will happen that will cause a call for government solutions. The public by and large does not have the time to research what those government solutions are, or what they would actually do, and, once government regulations are passed, the public tends to move on to other things.

Special interests, on the other hand, take the long view; they know *exactly* what government activities affect them, and they know exactly *how they are affected*. Each company has a *special* interest in whatever industries it operates, and companies continue to lobby to have government do things that are favorable to them, *long after the public has moved on to other things*.

Companies don't let the wording of regulations dissuade them – they can lobby regulatory bodies to interpret regulations to do whatever they want them to do, quite independently of what the regulations actually say. Just as politicians and judges can say that the phrase "the right of the people to keep and bear arms shall not be infringed" allows the government to arm the military and provides no right for *the people* to keep and bear arms, so too can regulatory agencies interpret regulations to mean anything they want them to mean. *Unlike* with the right to bear arms, one will find little opposition to creative interpretations of obscure regulations nobody has read. Regulatory bureaucrats are not elected.

Do not overlook state and local governments either, and particularly if in a small or medium-sized business. State and local governments spend a tremendous amount of money on things like roads, bridges, schools, parks, and universities. There is ample opportunity to use these projects for a company's advantage, and it may cost less to bribe state and local governments than to bribe the federal government. Many of the regulatory agencies in the federal government exist separately in each individual state. If something can't be regulated by a federal agency, companies may be able to get it done in the state(s) where they operate.

TAX FARMING?

Local taxes can be a treasure trove, both on the spending side, as well as on the paying side. If a company has a plant that employs a few hundred people, that company can open negotiations in Mexico to relocate, and then extort state and local governments to give grants and tax breaks to keep the company from leaving. Just tell them, "Our community means so much to me that if I can just stay profitable while staying here, I will do so." If a company has multiple plants or multiple businesses, it is not hard to move profits around to make a given plant, or a subsidiary business, look unprofitable, even if that plant, or subsidiary, makes a lot of money. When I worked for a compression sprayer company, we were a subsidiary of a larger company, and we bought many of our components from other subsidiaries of the same parent. We paid far more for some components than normal market prices, making us less profitable (on paper), and the other subsidiaries more profitable, at any given point in time.

Extorting local governments by threatening to leave is legal, and effective.

Most of the public thinks that as long as we elect representatives to represent us, then "we the people" are in charge. The truth is that unelected bureaucrats are in charge, and the power of government can very easily be purchased and exploited, to allow companies to earn profits they would *never* be able to earn in a free market. All it requires is a little imagination, and judicious use of money.

Don't worry about the money it costs either. As long as a company is successful (and if that company spends enough on bribes,[3] success is almost assured) it will get the money back in higher profits. When a company invests in better goods and services for the public to consume, that company is investing its own money, but when a company invests in government cronyism, at the end of the day it is the taxpayer who pays. Government is the only entity in the world that can be bribed with it's own money.

Companies can hire people to assist in these endeavors as well. Our business schools churn out MBAs, all of whom are trained in both free-market ways to earn profits and in ways to use government to earn profits.

The bottom line is, it is hard making goods and services people want, whereas it is very easy for a company to bribe the government to fleece the public on the company's behalf. If making money is the only thing that matters, hire some MBAs, and reach into the sewage pit of government bureaucracy. Doing so leads to dirty hands, but it can also make someone rich.

In Jim McKelvey's book *The Innovation Stack*, he tells of how Federal Regulation of the airline industry protected high fare prices and poor service for decades. Then along came Herb Kelleher of Southwest Airlines who challenged this oligopoly all the way to the Supreme Court. Ironically, Southwest did not take customers away from the established airlines - it took them away from Greyhound Bus lines with cheap fares. Who benefited? The customer.

The great irony about this sad state of affairs is that many people think the solution is to have even more government involvement. These people are very vocal, and they permeate our colleges, so with every generation the call for more government cronyism gets louder. They don't call it "cronyism" (they prefer the phrase "mixed economy") but cronyism is what it is.

Consider the phrase, "Trickle-Down Economics." This phrase is generally used to refer to free-market capitalism, but does money "trickle down" under free-market mechanics? No. In free markets, each person earns what they can, and keeps what they earn. There is no magic centralized pot of money for wealth to "trickle down" from.

A more accurate phrase was coined by President John F. Kennedy when he reduced taxes: "A rising tide floats all boats." When everyone keeps more of the money they make, it is a metaphorical rising tide of money, benefitting everyone who works for a living.

Now consider socialism. In its purest form, under socialism, government seizes all income and earnings, and spends that money however the government rulers see fit. The hope in such a system is that some of the money will "trickle back down" to those who earned it (Exhibit A: North Korea, where the people subsist on a diet of oatmeal, cornmeal, and pine bark.)

Cronyism (often called "crony capitalism") is an economy in which the economic elite purchase the government, and then use government power to centrally control the economy, for the benefit of the economic elite.

How is this functionally any different from socialism, in which the political elite overthrows the economic elite, and then centrally plans the economy for their *own* benefit (Exhibit B: Venezuela, where the people are starving)?

Under free markets, government lacks the power to centrally plan the economy for *anyone's* interests. Each person, and each business, must do things that benefit customers, if they want to make any money at all. In free markets, competition forces businesses to focus on things the customer wants.

An economy can be easily defined as the sum total of all production and consumption. Cronyism and socialism both attempt to control consumption and production, but in all cases, an economy has real people, with real needs, and real wants. The demand of real people, acting in their own self-interest in pursuit of their individual needs and wants, is the organic part of the economy.

In a free market, the customer is in control, rather than the government, or Economic elites. Companies who do not give customers what they want shrink, or go out of business, as Kodak did. Kodak invented the digital camera, but did not push the digital camera to market. Customers wanted digital cameras, and bought them from Kodak's competitors, such as Canon. Kodak is now out of the camera business.

Using cronyist techniques will not help our nation, nor the world economy. The profit one makes off the backs of the taxpayer reduces the efficiency of our economy, harming the taxpayer directly, through a higher tax burden and higher prices, and indirectly, through a smaller economy with lower paying jobs. I can't say that the corrupt way does not work, however, because it does, and as long as the public keeps looking for government "protection" from a system already gamed by too-much government "protection," the public will continue to demand an ever larger and more powerful government, whose powers go to the highest bidder.

If a company does decide to take advantage of graft and corruption, I offer a warning: control is an illusion. The political winds are fickle, and they can turn on a dime, as Solyndra learned.

If a company *still* wants to use cronyism, I just showed how to do it, so read no further. The rest of this book is not about cronyism; it is about making money the honest way – by making better goods and services than do competitors, and by meeting the needs of customers better than anyone else. This book is about understanding "value," and streamlining everything done to provide as much value as possible. Who decides what is value? Customers decide. You and I decide, rather than politicians and their elite business cronies.

Competition in free markets makes the country a better place. Companies may get driven out of business, and people may lose jobs, but this kind of economic churn is healthy for the nation, as it frees up resources (including labor) which can then be used in other ways that provide more value. In this way, the LP record was replaced by the cassette, which was in turn replaced by the CD, which was replaced by the MP3. Today, streaming music has replaced the MP3.

There will be those who will say that we need to move past the point where we have an economy based on competition; that we need to build a country, or a community (ideally a world community), based on cooperation for the public good. To them I say, I am a member of the public, and I will decide for myself what is "good" in my own life. The "public good" is by definition what is good for the public, of which we are all members, so the "public good" is also the composite "good" of each individual. No one person has a right to choose what is "good" for someone else. Each person knows what is best for themselves.

While there are some things that are better provided collaboratively, such as roads and police protection, most things are best provided through healthy competition in free and open markets. We should not continue building the bureaucratic nightmare that gets used by private companies to fleece the public, but should allow each individual person, and each individual company, to pursue their own interests and desires however they wish, provided that they do not infringe upon the rights of others. This is an approach in which companies have no choice but to make money by better fulfilling the needs of customers than do others.

In a free-market system, the consumer thrives, and we are all consumers.

NOTES

1 *Executive Greed*, Vinay B. Kothari, Palgrave Macmillian, 2010.
2 *The Innovation Stack*, Jim McKelvey, Penguin Random House, 2020.
3 Bribes are not obvious cash payments. Bribes are money-laundered by hiring the politician's relatives, or by paying a politician's 'speaker fees,' or by donations to 'Foundations' that in turn pay the politician.

2

The Limits of Demand and Systems Thinking

Systems thinking came out of Japan. It was the brain-child of W. Edwards Deming, who was an American quality expert during World War II. Deming's ideas found little support in the United States after the war, with American companies facing what seemed like limitless demand. When companies can sell whatever they can produce, at any quantity level, mass manufacturing techniques seem very practical. Japan, after the war, was in a very poor position to compete using mass manufacturing and had to find something other than efficiencies of scale to use as a competitive advantage. Deming taught them to work on the efficiency of each individual build rather than worrying about efficiencies of scale.

EFFICIENCIES OF SCALE VS. EFFICIENCIES OF BUILD

Efficiencies of scale and efficiencies of build are largely the opposite of one another. When working on efficiencies of scale, the focus is on building as many of something as possible. If a press presses out the metal shell of a car door, mass manufacturing says to run as many of the same door as possible before changing, to minimize change-over time, and to make more doors. When focusing on the efficiency of each individual build, on the other hand, it makes no sense to build a car door until one is needed, and building 1,500 of the same door in a row makes no sense at all. When looking at the efficiency of each build it makes sense to build only what is needed, when it is needed. How quickly a press can change from building one kind of door to another becomes far more important than how many of the same door a press can crank out in a row.

There is a lot of waste baked into mass manufacturing operations, but as long as a company can sell more of whatever it produces, it can spread the cost of that waste out over a growing level of production to keep per unit costs low. Once a company using mass manufacturing stops growing, and sees its sales start to shrink, suddenly all of the waste baked into mass manufacturing can't be spread out the same way, and costs per unit explode.

As an example, let us say that I expect to sell 7,500 cars over the next year, and I have $7,500,000 of waste baked into my mass manufacturing process. My cost for that waste would be $1,000 per car. If my demand seems unlimited, I can cut that waste simply by building 15,000 cars instead of 7,500, reducing my waste to $500 per car. To reduce the waste to $250 per car, I need only ramp up production to 30,000 cars. With unlimited demand, I can always reduce waste costs, per car, by building more cars. If I find, however, that I have $7,500,000 in waste and suddenly I cannot sell 7,500 cars, my waste per car begins to rise, and unless I can find a way to sell more, rather than fewer, cars, my competitive position declines.

This is, of course, a very simple example, and the costs associated with mass manufacturing are not static (some wastes – but not all – rise as production rises), but the whole point of mass manufacturing is that production grows faster than the cost of waste, and that is true *only until there are not more sales to be had.*

It is very common for mass manufacturing companies to grow like juggernauts until they suddenly can't spread their waste out over a growing number of units, and then they shrink, often with remarkable speed, such as happened with Chrysler and GM, in the 1980s.

As another example, imagine a mass manufacturing company that is thinking about replacing a manual production line with robots. Robots are very expensive, but they can produce without breaks or vacations, around the clock. How would a company decide whether or not to make the investment? Usually they would look at the cost of the manual process, per part, against the automated process, per part. Because the automated process is capable of making many more units, its per part costs are likely much lower than the manual process, and the investment may look like a good idea. This company would then figure out exactly how many units the automated process has to produce to keep its per part costs below the manual process, and would be careful to always run the automated process above that level.

UNSOLD INVENTORY = EXTRA WASTE

What if a company can't sell all of the parts the automated process needs to produce for it to be cheaper than manual labor? In that case, the company might build to inventory in the hope of more sales in the future, but what if those additional sales never materialize? What if sales start to decline?

If a company cannot sell all of the parts it produces, what it *should* do is to take all of the costs associated with all of the parts that did not sell, add in the costs of storing those unsold parts, and then spread all the costs of the unsold parts across the parts that did sell. If mass-manufacturing companies did this, their per part costs would explode.

Somewhere there is a controller reading this who wants to throw something at me. Inventory is an asset for a reason: it has value. The implicit assumption in assigning inventory value, however, is that at some point what was produced will be sold. If the only way to show a profit, even on paper, is to produce faster than a company can sell, that's a problem. Paper profits are often not real.

Another phrase some people will have a problem with is "limits of demand." There is no inherent limit to demand. Companies can always make new products, or make changes to existing products, to increase demand. If, however, we think of time in buckets, as we often do in business (fiscal quarter, fiscal year, etc.), each of those buckets represents what happened during a specific time period. *Within* each time period, a company only makes money on what it sells. Producing beyond what you sell is to gamble on *future* sales.

In the case of General Motors at its peak, the gamble stopped paying off. With competitors eating at market share, suddenly GM had fewer cars selling every quarter. Building inventory, and counting it as an "asset," did not improve cash flow, and could not fix the problem. GM imploded.

We see this story repeated often – it is the reason so many companies implode right as they zenith, and I dare say General Motors would have gone out of business (along with the rest of the Big Three) on several occasions had it not been for government bailouts.

Toyota is reaching the limit of demand for its cars now, and has actually been overtaken by Volkswagen as the largest automotive manufacturer in the world, but because Toyota focused on making each *build* more efficient, rather than focusing on efficiencies of scale, hitting the limit of demand made very little difference to Toyota's ongoing operations. Toyota is well positioned to take the lead back from Volkswagen, and could very easily push their demand curve upward again. Implosion is not on the horizon.

Toyota practices what is called "Systems Thinking."

Systems thinking can be difficult. We tend to look at systems in isolation, and I have been as guilty of that as anyone. I was once the IT Manager for a company that made lawn and garden sprayers, and as a young IT Manager, just out of the Army, I tried to run the IT department as efficiently as possible, because that is what a good manager does. But what is "efficient"? If I provided the company with the IT systems and resources it needed at minimal cost, would that have been "efficient," or is it possible that internal efficiencies in the IT department may increase costs elsewhere in the organization?

SAVING A COMPANY OUT OF BUSINESS?

The answer is that internal efficiencies in one department can absolutely come at the expense of the overall organization. Systems theory calls this "sub-optimization." An IT department may be at its most efficient if it only runs one database, but a database designed to hold every transaction – every purchase order and invoice, every material transfer and inventory movement, every sales order and shipping notice – will run very slowly when crunching numbers for a sales report. In the quest to find the "one database that does everything," an IT Manager might save a few tens of thousands of dollars, but it might cost millions in lost sales. With such savings, it is possible to save a company right out of business. Luckily the company I worked for back then had a number of more experienced managers who were able to prevent me from making too many youthful mistakes!

We've all heard horror stories where one department wanted to eliminate something that cost, say, $100 per item produced, but doing so would cost $1 per item in another department, and was turned down. The manager who refused to take a $1 per item hit, when it would have saved $100 per item elsewhere, was thinking about internal efficiencies, and was sacrificing overall efficiencies in the process. She was sub-optimizing her department at the expense of the overall company. This is the opposite of systems thinking.

Everything everyone does requires inputs, and produces outputs. When receiving inputs, one is acting in a customer role. When sending outputs, one is acting in a supplier role. We are both suppliers and customers in everything we do, and *our* suppliers and customers are often *within our own organizations*. We have to learn to look at internal customers as if they are just as important as external customers, and we have to learn to challenge internal suppliers, to allow them to better meet our needs, even when our internal suppliers may also be our managers.

ALIGNMENT: GIVING THE NEXT OPERATION WHAT THEY NEED

To be aligned is to be synchronized with others in pursuit of a larger purpose or meaning. A circuit on a circuit board is aligned when its operation helps the rest of the board function correctly. A worker on a production line is aligned when his or her job helps to create a finished product as efficiently as possible.

A company is only aligned when it is providing some valuable good or service that the larger society needs, or wants. The words "alignment" and "value" are thus inexorably linked; a worker is aligned when they provide value, and the more value a worker provides, the better they are aligned.

Alignment occurs at every level of an organization, but it is often very hard to see. When a worker on a production line is not aligned, it is relatively easy to see, because the next person in line does not get what they need to perform their task (you may see parts piling up at that work station), but when there is a lack of alignment between lines, or between different parts of a company that are not on production lines, it can be far more difficult to spot.

When we are in a customer role, it is important that we communicate to our suppliers what our true needs are. We should constantly look at what we get from suppliers, and see if we can find ways to improve that input. We must then communicate those improvements to our suppliers, and work with them to help them make those improvements. When we are in a supplier role, even if we are the CEO of our organization, we must be sensitive to the needs of our internal customers and must be willing to adapt to better meet those needs. One definition of a CEO's job is to provide what her subordinates need to do their jobs.

SIPOC: SUPPLIERS, INPUTS, PROCESS, OUTPUTS, CUSTOMERS

The acronym "SIPOC", which stands for "Suppliers, Inputs, Process, Outputs, Customers," illustrates how to think in terms of systems, and companies can diagram out processes using SIPOC as a model. SIPOC meetings involve everyone involved in a process, including suppliers and customers of the process, working to re-engineer the process.

In a SIPOC meeting, a company takes a process and lists out all suppliers (both internal and external). For each supplier, all of the inputs are listed. The mechanics of the process are defined next, followed by the outputs the process creates. Finally, how the customers of that process use the outputs is described.

After going forward through the process from supplier to customer, the process is repeated in reverse (from customer to supplier). The customers are encouraged to look at what they do, and to think of how the outputs could be improved to better enable them to do their jobs. The process is looked at to see what changes could be made to produce what the customers want. Inputs invariably are changed to support the new process, and this filters back down to the suppliers, whose jobs change to produce better inputs.

SIPOC meetings work. The process is simple, but effective, and if companies run SIPOC meetings, starting with external customers, and working backward, through operations until reaching external suppliers, companies cannot help but to streamline everything they do. Most lean people focus on another modeling technique discussed throughout this book, called Value Stream Mapping. I focus on both techniques. SIPOC and Value Stream Mapping are complimentary – SIPOC methodology helping to improve the Value Stream Mapping process.

SHAREHOLDER VALUE IS PRODUCED BY GIVING VALUE TO THE CUSTOMER

Businesses, we are told, exist to create shareholder value – to make money for those who own them. Milton Freidman said that this is the *only* reason businesses exist. Indeed, it is true: businesses do exist to make money for the people who own them, but to leave that statement as is, breaks with the larger truth about *how* businesses make money.

The fact is that nothing exists in isolation. As individuals we affect, and are affected by, everything we touch. We are not solitary creatures, but parts of a larger society (a system). As businesses, we are a part of a larger society as well – a society with segments that either do, or do not, need the goods and services we produce. If we produce goods and services societal segments want, it becomes easy to make money. Profit is a natural byproduct of the value-adding company. The more value we add, the more profit we will make.

If we do something that society wants, but that costs more to make than society is willing to pay for it (and are losing money instead of making a profit), then we are not really adding value, but are destroying it. Adding value is the *only* way to make profit in a truly free market.

Generally, people who do not like free markets, and who read that last paragraph, will mention things like snake oil salesmen, who make money by fooling people into wasting their money on garbage. It is true that someone can make money, for a short period of time, with schemes, but people catch on to these schemes and become harder to fool again, which is why snake oil salesmen are always moving. Also, snake oil salesmen are succeeding through inefficiencies in the market. In a truly efficient market, the seller and buyer both know the same things – such as that snake oil does not work. The internet has made it easier for buyers to know as much as sellers.

THINKING OUTSIDE OF THE BOWL

There is no concept in this book that is more important than the notion that nothing exists in isolation. Everything exists as a part of a larger system. Even a goldfish in a fish bowl is a part of a larger system. A goldfish bowl has, if nothing else, the bowl, the fish, and water. If the fish is not fed, it dies. This system is affected by the ambient temperature of the room it is in, the amount of light, and countless other factors.

A goldfish in a bowl is a very simple system, but it is still a system, and it exists as a part of a larger system, with an owner that chose to buy it. The goldfish bowl needed to be made in a factory, and whomever made it had to buy materials. The food the fish is fed had to be produced out of materials that were grown by a company specializing in fish-foods. These companies employ people. Those people have lives and families that depend on the need to buy goldfish, bowls, and goldfish food, for their own livelihood. It is likely that some of the people working to make goldfish bowls and fish food also buy goods and services from the company that employs the goldfish owner. All of these systems are interrelated, and if a company wants to be more successful than its competitors, that company has to interrelate to the larger systems better than its competitors do. Only then is that company truly thinking in terms of systems.

Systems thinking can be applied at any level, throughout any organization. Any employee in any organization can seek out those who utilize their outputs and ask, "What changes could I make in what I produce to make your job easier?" The person who asks this question will generally find out that much of what they produce is not needed, and that what they produce needs to be modified before it can be used. In other words, improvements can be made. It takes a manager at some level to call an actual SIPOC meeting, but anyone can seek out those who use their outputs and ask what they can do to improve. Everyone at every level of an organization can seek to better fit in with the systems with which they interact.

As an example, say Worker A polished a part she made before giving it to Worker B (her customer in the SIPOC chain). One day Worker B remarks that polishing was not needed – the part was not visible in the finished machine, and the part exerts no friction on other parts. This process can be improved by having Worker A stop polishing the part. Suddenly less work needs to be performed.

3

Layoffs, Trust, and Changing Cultures

We've all been there: the market hits a downturn and we have too much capacity, and too much staff, to weather the storm.

This book is based on the idea that the right culture is the biggest strategic asset a company can have. In the right culture, companies can never, ever, under any circumstances, lay anyone off. If a company has too much staff, the company can reduce it through attrition, by not replacing people who retire or leave of their own accord; it can move people between roles (and if they leave because they don't like the new role, that's on them); and it can always fire for cause (most companies have people they avoid firing even though they have cause); but no company that wants to change its culture, can ever lay anyone off. Ever. The layoff should be placed in the dust bin of history (but don't worry – I'll discuss an alternative later in this chapter).

Why? A successful culture involves trust, and if a company's employees do not trust that they will benefit, should they improve the company, they will not help the company improve. They will instead create defensive tasks that provide no value, but that make them look busy. Employees who are afraid of losing their jobs fight change; nobody wants to improve themselves out of a job.

I once worked as an on-site consultant for a company that had a programmer who intentionally made all of his programs as convoluted as possible, in the belief that if nobody understood how they worked, the company would never be able to let him go. This guy had all kinds of complex cross-reference tables his programs would needlessly consult, just to make processes harder to maintain, and to make his importance seem greater than it really was. He made himself, quite literally, the "keeper of the process." He was eventually laid off anyway, and the company struggled a great deal working around the weight of all of those complex programs that nobody knew how to maintain. I can't even begin to describe how much money was wasted as a result.

On the other end of the spectrum, imagine an employee discovering, after doing a value-stream map, that their current role adds no value to the organization; that everything they do, the company not only could do without, but would be better off doing without. If you don't need the work an employee performs, you don't need the employee in that role.

In most organizations, the employee would try to hide that he or she adds no value at all, and would try to find ways to add the appearance of value through the creation of defensive tasks. What one wants this employee to do, is to walk right up to their manager, and tell their manager that the employee's role can be eliminated. No employee will do that if they believe that *they* will also be eliminated. Companies need employees who constantly look at how they can improve their jobs, removing waste from what they do, and finding new ways or new roles they can perform, to add more value to the organization. Companies need employees who constantly move themselves from non-value-adding activities, to value-adding activities.

Even if this hypothetical employee was wrong, and they really did add value, the company wants employees that ask hard questions, and who not only actively, but aggressively evaluate their roles. Employees willing to tell their managers that they don't add enough value, and who want to be repurposed so they can add more value, are exactly the kinds of employees a company should want, and these are the kinds of employees this book is designed to foster. As soon as a company lays employees off, any interest their employees may have had in improving their company, or their role within it, ends, making the organization nothing more than a means to a paycheck.

Even if a company has too many employees, whatever short term gain that company can get from laying people off will always be more than offset by the long-term pain layoffs cause.

The collective efforts of a company's employees act like a river, and as soon as employees think they are expendable, the current begins to flow in the wrong direction. A company can swim against that current, and if the company is fast enough, it may even make progress. If all of the firm's competitors have the same issues (and they probably do) then this company may be able to beat its competitors, even while swimming against the current, but would it not be much easier to gain ground if the company could swim *with* the current?

PUT YOUR TEAM FIRST AND THE CURRENT FLOWS YOUR WAY

The culture of one's organization – the flow of the water in which a company swims – is more important than any customer, any project, any product, any department, or any single employee, including the CEO. When I was in the Marine Corps, I had a Commanding Officer who told us that while he was the highest-ranking person in the unit, collectively we outranked him many times over. He did not just say that either; his actions showed that he meant it.

I had another commanding officer, this one in the Army, whom I consider the finest officer I ever served under. I don't remember him ever telling us that the unit was more important than its commander, but he treated us as if the unit was more important than he was, and we would have not only followed him into the depths of Hell, but scared the holy hell out of Satan in the process.

As a general rule, the officers in the Marine Corps are better than the officers in the Army, and the worst officers in the Army are generally those who went to West Point. Marines are taught that being a Marine – the title itself – is more important than life, and as Marines, they are treated with a level of dignity and respect by their superiors, that other branches cannot touch. Perhaps the Army Rangers and other special forces can match this, but in general the Army cannot.

I had a Platoon Leader in the Army who exemplified the typical Army officer. We were on a training exercise, supporting a tank unit that was generally supported by other engineers. As a rule, Combat Engineers in the field are fed by the units they support, but this particular tank unit told our platoon leader we were on our own for food, and as a consequence we did not eat for over a week.

I was not a light Combat Engineer, but a heavy Combat Engineer. We drove tanks modified for engineering duties, and having tanks, we also had plenty of room to bring extra things, like snack foods (which we called "Pogey Bait"). For the first few days, we consumed our snack foods. Some of the snacks were even marginally dinner-like. After a while, however, we were out of Pogey Bait, and then we went hungry.

Around dinner time one day, our Platoon Sergeant got a bead on some food and sent a Humvee to go pick it up for us. Our Platoon Leader was furious. He chased down that Humvee and turned it around to go pickup Concertina Wire (a military barbed wire) instead.

What this Second Lieutenant knew was that his performance was the only thing that would determine when and if he became a Captain. Once an officer hits Captain, only half are promoted to Major. Only half of all Majors are promoted to Lieutenant Colonels, and so on up the rest of the officer structure. Being a very competitive field, Army officers tended to put their careers ahead of their soldiers.

That would have never have happened in the Marine Corps. The Marine Corps may have the same promotion system (I don't know whether they do or not), but Marine officers are by and large anal about taking care of their Marines. The idea of chasing down a Humvee that was going for food, and repurposing it for something else, would never even occur to a Marine officer, unless another food source was readily available. To a Marine, the idea of letting fellow Marines go hungry in a training exercise is unconscionable. Even in war, Marines would rather attack the enemy and take *their* food than go hungry!

People sometimes ask me who I would rather go into combat with between the Army and the Marine Corps. I would rather go to combat with the Charlie Company, 82nd Engineer Battalion I served with in Bamberg, Germany, under the Commanding Officer I mentioned earlier (should he read this, he'll know who he is, so "Blue Babe Sir!"), but by and large it is not even a valid question: The Marine Corps would be *vastly* preferable.

The difference between the Marine Corps and the Army, and the difference between most Army units and the Charlie Company, 82nd Engineer Battalion I served in, was all about culture. The culture of strong units is based on the knowledge that the people in the unit, and the things they do, matter to their leadership.

It should be obvious that I prefer the Marine Corps to the Army, but the best *unit* I was in was the one with the best *leader*, and that was in the Army. There is a lesson in that fact.

LEADERS LEAD WITH ACTIONS, NOT WORDS

Culture matters, and leaders control culture through their actions, not their words. Words matter too, but only if they are backed-up by actions.

A culture of employees who honestly believe that they are valued, not just because of the roll they currently play, but because they matter in the broader sense, will be willing to do things other employees would not do. They will treat their employer like family, and will sacrifice (and fight) to protect their employer, the way they would sacrifice and fight to protect their family. In a sense, all of the employees become a family, looking to the leadership for guidance, and doing their utmost to carry that guidance out. Having such a culture is infinitely more valuable than saving a little money, or improving some metric like "Revenue Per Employee," and no company will ever build such a culture unless its organization permeates trust.

Layoffs are like wasp spray to trust, and anyone who has ever sprayed wasps knows what I mean: one can literally watch the trust fall off as the layoffs hit the nest.

That said, there are times when a company has to let people go because of a downturn, and there is no way around that. The way to handle this is by maintaining 10% of the workforce as temporary workers. These workers know they may be let go at any time for any reason, but they will want to become full-time employees, and will be motivated by the possibility that they may one day be hired in. The company can let them go without affecting the morale of its full-time employees, and when the company brings them back, they will be just as motivated as before, knowing that if they work hard and get hired full time, they too will be protected.

If 10% of a company's workforce are temps, the company will always have a pool of known employees to look through for any permanent positions that become available. A known commodity is always better than an unknown, and once a company has a reputation as a great place to work, that company will have no problem finding eager temps looking to join the temp-pool. On top of that, when a company has a temp it does not like, the company will find that temps are easier to let go.

Companies will be tempted to hire-in really good temps even when there are no full-time roles available (without reducing the temp pool to less than 10% of the workforce). If someone succumbs even once to the temptation of hiring someone before there truly is a place for them, they will be tempted to do it again and again. Soon the company temp pool will be 8% of the workforce, and then 5%. Suddenly a recession will hit, the company won't have enough temps, and there will be pressure to layoff full-time employees. Don't let that happen. A company can tell a temp that it wants to keep them, and that it will hire them in when it can, but a company cannot hire them in until they can do so and still have 10% of their workers as temps.

Someone is going to call the practice of having "permatemps," "Machiavellian." Perhaps it is, but Machiavelli was not immoral, so much as amoral. Machiavelli's book, *The Prince*,[1] was brutal in its logic, but it was also very logical, and not everything in it was bad. As a consequence, even if having "permatemps" sounds Machiavellian, do it anyway. The purpose of having a pool of temps is to protect permanent employees, who never get laid off, and when there is a permanent position to fill, there will be temps waiting to take it. Not laying off employees is a very positive thing, and as long as the company is open about its practices, there is nothing unethical about having a constant pool of temps.

As an example, renters and homeowners use "temps" all the time when they make repair and/or service calls. A homeowner may call in a plumber to replace a toilet, when in a downturn that homeowner might decide to do that same work themselves.

Nobody forces a temp to be a temp; they do that by choice. If someone wants to work for a particular company as a temp, based on the hope of one day being a full-time employee in that company, that is their choice, and if they value that choice, it is because they feel that it is the best option they have available to them. Who is someone else – a third party – to criticize a company for providing what is a mutually beneficial arrangement, for both the company, and the employee? If a company wants, it can even hire from a temp agency that provides benefits. The goal is not to have a pool of employees to treat poorly, but to be able to downsize, without damaging the culture of the organization.

Try to spread the temps out as much as possible, but spread them out strategically rather than evenly. Companies should look at each department, and define various staffing levels for different demand cycles. Temps should be put in roles a company can do without in a downturn (like roles more than one person fills), so that when downturns come, the company can scale back accordingly.

Layoffs are almost always done haphazardly by managers who seem surprised that a downturn has occurred, but downturns do occasionally occur, and managers should only be surprised by the specific timing and/or the specific severity. Ideally how one responds to a downturn is planned. A company probably doesn't want to share the specifics of its downturn plans with people who do not need to know them, but department heads should know exactly how to respond, in their respective departments, to downturns of various magnitudes.

Strategically planning for layoffs is another thing people will call "Machiavellian." Companies who do this will be accused of "playing with people's lives." My response is that this is not playing with people's lives, but only their livelihoods, which is a necessary part of running a business, and that laying permanent employees off – which is avoided – is also a way to play with lives, but in a more haphazard and costly way. Having temps, and laying temps off strategically, does the least amount of harm to the fewest people, and keeps the company culture strong so that the company can rebound quickly when the downturn ends.

"10% of employees being temps" is, incidentally, not a firm number. Each company is different, and as a company builds strategic downturn plans, they might find that their ideal target number is higher, or lower, than 10%. The important thing is that the number be determined strategically.

Also note that companies need to periodically look at their downturn plans. Companies that follow this book will be improving constantly, making their downturn plans obsolete over time. With every aspect of a business falling into a state of constant improvement, downturn plans will have to be improved as well.

Scaling back up once the downturn ends will be less of a problem, as the techniques in this book will allow companies to continuously do more with fewer people. During expansions, companies will not need to add as many people as were let go. Employees learn to do more with less, allowing recessions to make companies stronger.

Note that this also means it will be challenging to get back to a 10% level of temps after a recession ends. Companies will have to do that through attrition, as employees leave on their own.

Explain to employees that they may have to change roles. While no company wants to change anyone's role against their wishes, companies will do what they have to do to remain competitive, and will mandate people adopt new roles when necessary. If someone voluntarily leaves an organization rather than change roles, they are better off elsewhere, and the company is better off without them.

If a company has had layoffs in the past, then don't expect employees to trust that the company will not use layoffs in the future. Talk is cheap, and employees will be highly skeptical.

Note too that though layoffs kill any positive culture in an organization, not having layoffs does not in and of itself create a winning culture. The rest of the items in this book are necessary to do that. Avoiding layoffs only eliminates the biggest culture-killing threat.

The company culture will not change right away either, and many employees (typically about a third) will be so against the cultural changes, as they *do* start to emerge, that they will leave the organization rather than adapt. Let them go. Some of them will be key contributors some might not think the company can do without. The company, however, *can* do without them, or at least the company can *replace* them. No employee is as important as the overall culture of an organization, so don't keep anyone who won't come onboard. Also, as employees are lost because of cultural changes, the company can start to build a pool of temps.

TREATING YOUR TEAM LIKE FAMILY IS A COMPETITIVE ADVANTAGE

Letting employees go, and then replacing some of them with temps, will accomplish two things: first, it tells employees that the company really is serious about changing its culture, and second (perhaps more importantly), replacing people who leave with temps sends the message that the company really means it when managers say there will never be a layoff of permanent personnel again.

Some of the people who will fight cultural changes the most will be managers, including some executives. One *really* needs to let them go. Senior executives are generally too smart to openly challenge cultural changes, but they'll use passive-aggressive tactics to try to make the cultural changes fail. Watch for that, and fire the offenders. Give no second chances with executives; be decisive.

At the same time, reward those who begin to adapt to the new culture. Some will do so quickly, whereas others will follow. There will be a lot of fence sitters who won't know which way to go until the new prevailing culture begins to win.

If a plant (or location) is being shut-down, offer jobs in other plants, or other locations, to anyone who wants one. Most will not take the company up on relocating, and particularly if relocation assistance is not offered, but employees will notice, and will appreciate the willingness to relocate people rather than laying them off, as it means the company is keeping its word.

There is an old saying that employees are family. Embrace that. Keep anyone who is loyal, and get to know them and what goes on in their lives. Don't do that just to impress them either – actually care about them and how they are doing, and encourage them to care about each other. Some companies have been known to lose money on orders during the off season to keep their talented team together. They know that when orders pick up, that team will produce great products at a profit.

NOTE

1 *The Prince*, Niccolo Machiavelli, Antonia Blado d'Asola, 1513.

4

Automation and Bottlenecks

I was on a plant tour once where a very proud plant manager showed me a new, fully automated production line, that could produce things several times as quickly as the manual line it replaced. I remember asking how much money the company saved because of this line, and being told that, as expensive as the line was, as long as it was running at 85% efficiency (or higher), it was cheaper than using manual labor. As we walked through the rest of the plant, I noticed that large portions of the plant were working just to keep feeding the automated line, so they could keep it running above 85% efficiency. I also remember seeing forklifts taking the product coming out of the automated line, and taking it into trucks, to store it off-site.

The automated line did not make finished goods, but it did replace a number of workers, and to an accountant, as long as it was operating at 85% efficiency, it was better than manual labor, *even if the company could not use all the output from this line when it ran at 85% efficiency.* This plant was running itself ragged trying to keep an automated line running at a pace that greatly exceeded demand.

To an accountant, inventory is on the asset side of the balance sheet, meaning that it represents value, and thus wealth. To the accountant, I would say that inventory only represents wealth when it is sold as a part of a finished good, and building inventory is putting the proverbial cart ahead of the horse. One cannot get rich building inventory. One can only get rich selling the products one builds. Even if a company really is going to sell the inventory it builds, it is still better to build the finished goods as close to the time of sale as possible. My colleague, Mike McCarthy, tells me that every car built at the BMW plant in South Carolina is sold at a dealership before it is built. Result? Zero inventory assets, but tremendous cash flow.

What an accountant will understand (I hope) is the relationship between turns and inventory. If I have two machines that both harden steel, and one can harden steel twice as fast as the other (giving me half the batch size), the machine that runs twice as quickly is also, all else being equal, going to be twice as profitable.

Someone is going to mention that I am producing the same amount of steel, so the profit is the same, but the profitability of a process is not the same as the profit a process creates. Profitability is about taking an investment (in this case in steel billets) and turning it over to create profit. If I have a process that earns, say, $100,000 a year hardening steel, and I have to have $10,000 of steel in it at any given time to keep up with production, that part of my process is earning me ten times per year what I have to invest in it. If I can run it twice as quickly, and only need $5,000 of steel in it at a time, suddenly I am earning twice the return on my investment as before.

Retailers understand this phenomenon well. The number of times a retailer turns over their inventory is at least as important as how much they make each time they turn their inventory over. This is true not only in retail, but everywhere. One has to invest a certain amount in one's organization at any given time to make a certain amount of profit, and the total profitability of the whole operation is determined, both by the amount of profit earned each time inventory is turned over, as well as by the number of times inventory is turned over. If carried inventory is reduced, and sales stay the same, profitability grows.

Everyone understands how reducing some costs, such as labor and electricity, can save a company money. Work in process inventory should be treated no differently, but because it sits on the asset side of the balance sheet, many accountants treat it differently than other costs.

I get why accountants consider work in process inventory an "asset." Eventually it will be sold as a part of something, and the company will realize profit from it. What I want accountants to acknowledge is that building something before it is needed does not create any more profit than does waiting to build it until it is needed. Even in a capacity constrained, seasonal company, it behooves the company to produce no more ahead of time than absolutely necessary, to keep up during the company's busy season.

In our steel example, I only improved one process by a $5,000 reduction in total work-in-process inventory. That might sound trivial, but as inventory is removed from other processes, the savings add up. Consider the cost of *all* the work-in-process inventory in a company. What if the *entire amount* was reduced by half? Suddenly, real money is freed up, and that money can be invested in other things, such as increased production, or a second business venture, where it *does* become additional profit. There is also the space inventory takes up, which can be repurposed as additional manu-facturing space.

INCREASING INVENTORY TURNS = INCREASING CASH FLOW

Most companies outside of retail tend to disregard turns. They look at sales volumes, costs, and profits, but not inventory turns. Turns should be a part of the equation.

I was in a sales meeting once where a sales person was discussing how to sell a heat-treat oven that could heat steel twice as quickly as traditional machines. The sales people discussed savings from reduced energy costs, and all kinds of other soft savings, but somehow the concept of this oven needing to have half as much steel in it, at any given time, making it twice as profitable to run, never occurred to them, and they did not use that fact even after I explained it to them.

In the aggregate it makes sense: if I have a million dollars tied up into a business that makes two million dollars a year, then my return on that investment is 200%. If I have only $500,000 tied up, at any given time, and I still make $2 million, my return on investment is 400% – 400% cash return flowing through the business versus 200% cash return flowing through the business. There are of course costs tied up in the business other than work in process inventory, but work in process inventory is a big cost, and it makes sense to reduce it wherever one can.

Another reason why people struggle understanding that less inventory is a good thing is that they use traditional cost accounting, which consists of fixed, and variable, costs.

Fixed costs are those that are the same whether one item is produced, or a million items are produced. The CEO's salary is not apt to change based on how many of something is produced, so the CEO's salary is a fixed cost. Variable costs are those that change as more items are produced, such as the material costs of finished goods. Every business person knows that I can effectively reduce my fixed costs by producing more finished goods, and spreading my fixed costs out over more products. Every business person also knows that I can reduce my variable costs by reducing direct labor, by reducing material costs, or by doing anything else that makes a process cheaper to operate.

Unfortunately, it is never really that simple. Warehouse space is often held as a fixed cost, even though warehouses do not hold an equal amount of all items produced. Really, warehouse costs should be counted against only the items being stored, based on the storage costs for each item. Some customers are more expensive to deal with than others, and the fixed costs of dealing with difficult customers could be spread only over those items those customers purchase. There is a whole school of cost management called Activity Based Costing (and there is a very good book, titled *I May Be Wrong, But I Doubt It*, by Douglas T. Hicks[1]) covering how to more accurately account for costs than by using just Fixed and Variable costs. I won't get into detail about Activity Based Costing here, but suffice it to say that applying costs that only affect some products, across all products, has the effect of making some products appear to cost more to produce than they actually do, while making other products appear to cost less to produce than they actually do. This bad data leads to bad business decisions.

When an even spread of fixed costs makes a product seem to cost *less* than it really does, the result is often that the product is sold at a loss. When an even spread of fixed costs makes a product seem to cost *more* than it really does, the result is often that pricing is set too high, and sales are lost. Both scenarios reduce profitability. Activity-Based Costing can correct these issues.

COOKING FOUR STEAKS VS. FOUR HUNDRED

I got into an argument once with a professional chef friend of mine, about how to cook a steak. He cooks them on cast iron, first searing them on a stove, and then moving them into an oven to bake (he also sometimes bakes them first, and then sears them at the end). I grill them over charcoal. I said a charcoal grill is the way to go, and he said cast iron in an oven (after searing) is the way to go. Who is right?

My friend told me he knew better than me because he was a professional chef, and I am not, and that I should go with the way the pros use. A professional chef, however, is working for a restaurant that has cost and scale considerations I don't have at home. A professional chef is taught to cook based on a very different set of *constraints* than I face when cooking for my family. Does it not make sense that some things a professional chef has been taught are based on the constraints related to having to cook large amounts of food quickly, and not based on the flavor of the food?

For the record, I can cook a better steak than can a restaurant (to the point that I no longer enjoy steaks at restaurants). But then, with a family of four, I only have to cook four steaks, and I can wait for my grill to get as hot as possible before I throw the steaks on. A professional chef would never be able to make 400 steaks a night the way I cook them, and If I had to cook as many steaks as a professional chef, I could not do it at all.

Just like chefs, accountants have constraints. Everything they measure has a cost to measuring it. Accountants measure cost the way they do because, frankly, there are costs associated with measuring things more accurately. That said, modern computer technology has changed the equation such that it may make sense to use Activity Based Costing in places where it did not make sense in the past, and even where traditional cost accounting is used, the concepts of Activity Based Costing should be kept in mind.

Smaller batch sizes in any process are always preferable to bigger batch sizes, when all else is equal. An oven that can bake 50 parts in 30 minutes is always preferable to an oven that bakes 100 parts in an hour. A process that can heat-treat half as much steel twice as quickly as another process, will always be preferable, if all else is equal. Small batch sizes are a major tenet of lean manufacturing, with a goal of doing everything in one piece flow (with no batches at all).

Now that we've discussed the dangers of automation leading to extra work in process inventory, we can start to discuss what *to* automate. This requires knowing exactly what it is one's company does, and focusing on the parts of the company that in Lean parlance would be called the "Gemba."

The Gemba is operations. The Gemba is where the product or service is produced.

The Marine Corps has a phrase that illustrates what "Gemba" means, and that saying is, "If you aren't infantry, you're support." The infantry performs the value-adding operation of the Marine Corps (As General Norman Schwarzkopf put it, "killing people and breaking things"), and everyone else helps them do it. To the Marine Corps, infantry is the Gemba. Everyone else – even tankers who also "kill people and break things" – are acting in a supporting role to the infantry.

When I was in the Marine Corps, I was a Heavy Equipment Operator (I was a Combat Engineer in the Army). I was not in the Gemba. I supported the Gemba by making our infantry more mobile while making the enemy's infantry less mobile.

Companies should always focus on the Gemba. Allowing accounting to make business decisions, just to make the balance sheet look better (without making more money), allowing IT to use security as an excuse not to give employees (particularly employees in the Gemba) the access they need – anything that negatively affects the Gemba, directly or indirectly, is bad for business. To let a support role dictate doing something that hurts the Gemba is the epitome of stupid. That does not mean support people are stupid, but it means their specialized training *in support roles* often puts blinders on them, so that they cannot see the deeper importance of operations to the company *as a whole*.

In terms of systems thinking, the support departments sub-optimize their role, which results in operations as a whole not being optimized. A body is a system. What if the stomach got all the oxygen? The digestion role would certainly be (sub) optimized, but the heart muscles would be starved for oxygen and stop. The body would die. Each body sub-system needs to get the right amount of oxygen so that the total body is optimized.

Understanding how to *perform* a role represents "technical proficiency," whereas understanding how to *apply* a role to *better the Gemba* represents "tactical proficiency." Many people, particularly in support roles, are *technically* proficient, but not *tactically* proficient. Tactical proficiency includes understanding that the Gemba is where money is made, and thus, the Gemba is where one needs to focus. Everything else, be it artillery, tanks, airplanes, supply – whatever – is measured not on how well it runs internally, but on how well it supports the Gemba.

Accounting's role is to measure and advise, but they cannot be allowed to run the company. Nor can IT. Nor can Human Resources. And though the CEO *does* run the company (hopefully while listening to Operations), he or she had better be focused on the Gemba, and not something else. A CEO focusing on the wrong things can run a company into the ground, and there is nothing worse than a *CEO* who is not tactically proficient. The best CEOs are technically, tactically, and *strategically* proficient.

Support can improve the Gemba, as armored personnel carriers have improved the ability of Marine Infantry units to move around combat theatres. Those armored personnel carriers make the Marine Corps more efficient, by allowing the same number of troops to kill more people, and to break more things, than they could do if they were on foot all the time. As a combat engineer, I could create obstacles to prevent enemy troop movements, and could breech obstacles to allow more mobility to friendly forces – reducing the enemy's ability to kill people and break things, while enhancing the ability of friendly forces to kill people and break things. Similarly, when a company automates some processes on the plant floor, if that automation allows the company to make finished goods faster (and sales exist to support the increased speed), then it helps the Gemba. Conversely, if some robot helps a company make more work-in-process inventory pile up, then they are focusing on the wrong part of the Gemba, and/or they are not working on improving the Gemba at all. For more on this, study the Theory of Constraints in the book, *The Goal*,[2] discussed later in this chapter.

Support can often help other support roles be more efficient, but managers should always ask if they can tie that secondary efficiency back to the Gemba. Those things that improve the Gemba as an overall system should always be prioritized over those things that do not.

Some people think they can fully automate the Gemba, but I remember reading about a fully-automated auto plant GM lost its shirt on.

One major problem GM found was that if they did not catch quality problems as they were made, the plant could produce very large numbers of bad cars before anyone knew there was a problem. GM had to spend tons of money to repair those cars before they could be sold. *People* generally see problems whereas machines do not, and sensors can only catch *known* issues – not new ones, so chasing quality in a fully-automated system can be a pipe dream. Just ask Elon Musk, who struggles to automate his Tesla plants.

There is an even bigger problem with having too much automation. Let's say that some company does get all the kinks out of a fully automated plant. Let's say that this company builds car XYZ, and can suddenly produce flawless cars over and over again with zero defects, zero vacations, zero worker complaints, and zero payroll. Let's even assume that this company can sell cars as quickly as it can build them. The next year a competitor, who does not have a fully automated plant, introduces an improvement to a competing car, and suddenly our company has to weigh the risk of throwing their plant into turmoil again, trying to make the same improvement to their car, against the risk of losing market share for not making that change.

In the 1980s, Ford would use the previous year's sales as a given for the next year and would weigh any changes proposed against the assumption that if they changed nothing, they would repeat the previous year's sales. Somehow the notion that this was not a safe assumption was lost on them.

The big three waited over a decade to implement front-wheel drive in their cars, based on the costs of retooling existing plants to support front-wheel drive. The big three waited just as long to migrate to electro-static painting (that bonds the paint to the metal). Both of these things were HUGE improvements, and there are many similar examples of things our automotive companies would not do for a long time, even as they lost market share to foreign competitors who did those things.

These concerns are real. Does anyone really want to be tied to existing products *without the ability to change* because of a fear of breaking a plant? Is automation really helpful if it ties a company's hands?

We want to automate where it makes sense to do so, but we want to avoid automating in ways that act like a straight-jacket toward change in the Gemba. We want machines to make jobs easier, less dangerous, and less demeaning, but we want machines at a scale that allows us to change faster than our competitors can match. The things to automate are things that are dirty, dangerous, demeaning, or demanding.

I have never worked in, nor visited, a manufacturing operation that makes candies or other fully-automated food items, but I have seen videos of these things, and it appears that there may be a better argument for more automation in those environments. Tootsie Rolls do not change much year to year (which I am grateful for, being a Tootsie Roll fan!), so the fear of being handcuffed to automation may be less than in other industries. I would surmise, however, that even in this kind of environment, automation works best in areas that are dirty, dangerous, demeaning, or demanding, and that the reason more automation may work in these environments is that more tasks are dirty, dangerous, demeaning, or demanding.

Another thing to consider are root causes. I worked for a company that made injection-molded shutters, and I remember that when they would change colors, they had to bleed a tremendous amount of the old color of vinyl, to completely empty the lines, before going to the new color. This company prided itself in all of the different styles and colors of shutters it produced, but to keep up with the demand for all of those styles and colors, it had to keep massive warehousing space full of finished shutters.

Changing *styles* of shutters was an even bigger problem, as the mold had to cool down and be cleaned before it could be taken off, and a new mold could be put on the machine.

The solution the company came up with was to make tons of shutters in every conceivable style and color, and to store them as finished goods inventory. This made fulfilling orders a time-consuming process, with forklifts having to move from shutter to shutter across a very large amount of space. The company CIO wanted to create a warehouse inventory system to help speed up the process of fulfilling orders.

Really it was a slick system. The CIO wanted to be able to put shutters haphazardly in the warehouse, and then feed a picklist into a computer to have it route the forklift driver as quickly as possible in assembling orders. Since all of the product was essentially randomly distributed (and the computer knew where everything was), it was believed the company could minimize the distance the forklift would have to travel when picking an order. It sounded like a really smart project.

I had a chance to work on creating that system, but I was in the middle of my Lean Manufacturing studies, and I asked the wrong question: I asked if it would make more sense to work on reducing the need to have inventory. Someone else then created the inventory management system, and I was free to explore ways to reduce inventory requirements. I think the Chief Information Officer wanted me to spin my wheels on what he thought would be a worthless project.

Rather than spinning my wheels, I found that through a combination of rapid change-over, and statistics-based forecasting (which as luck would have it I was studying at that very moment), we could do better. I made a forecasting model in Excel that showed we could reduce inventories by at least 80%, even without rapid changeover. I showed it to my professor, and he loved it, so I began writing the forecasting model into the company's ERP system.

The company had two plants making shutters. We could have saved so much warehouse space in either of them (converting it to manufacturing space), that we could have shut one plant down completely. I unfortunately finished my MBA, and left the company, before implementing my fore-casting model (which was likely then scrapped), but it would have worked, and it is still an excellent example of how and where to automate. More importantly, it is an example of how to think through to the root cause, asking, in this case, not just, "How can we manage this inventory," but also, "Why do we need so much inventory?" Root-Cause Analysis is an important element of lean (discussed in more detail in the chapter on Strategic Decision Making), and I cannot stress enough the need to address *root* causes, particularly when automating.

One particular form of automation companies should focus on is that of Rapid Change Over.

Rapid Change Over tries to reduce the time it takes to do things like change shutter molds, or metal presses. The goal should be to reduce the time it takes to change a mold (and/or the color of shutters) down to the cycle time of one pair of shutters.

I was told that rapid change over was not possible with shutters, but plant managers in other industries have found ways to remove hot dies, such that they are cooled and cleaned offline. Running a second set of feed lines into a mold should have made it possible to cut one line off and start using a second one without running virgin vinyl through the machine. Solutions were possible, and those machines were a part of the company Gemba, so having them running waste, or sitting idle, was not very smart. These are things that should have been improved, and where automation could have been applicable.

AUTOMATE TO IMPROVE PROCESSES, NOT REDUCE PEOPLE

One should not automate to remove people, but to improve processes. If that means fewer people are needed, that's OK, but processes should be improved without regard for the impact on people. The goal is not "auto-mation," but "process improvement," and automation is only applicable when and where it improves processes. There may well be cases where

automation is possible, but where there are better ways to improve processes than to automate. I'm frequently surprised by how often I can
improve processes by *removing* automation.

One major problem with automation, when it does remove people, is that
machines cannot think. Because of this, automated processes use inspec-
tion to try and force quality into things after those things are produced.
Dr. Deming taught us that one cannot inspect quality into a process after
the fact. Quality must be a part of the process itself – each person in the
process being a quality manager who looks for defects. Unlike people,
automated processes can only look for *known* defects that may occur. A
laser may look for paint runs, for example. As long as a known defect
occurs in a known way, this can be effective, but what happens when a new
defect occurs, or an old defect occurs in a new way, which the automated
sensors are not designed to detect?

Where a company automates is also critical. Manufacturing systems have
bottlenecks that define the total output of the entire operation. Non-
manufacturing processes also have bottlenecks, but they are not always as
obvious, or as easy to find. Find those processes that determine the
throughput of the organization, and focus improvement efforts there.
Improving a process when the company already can't use all of its output
won't improve profitability, and nor will improving a process that is
starved for work.

THE THEORY OF CONSTRAINTS

Bottlenecks are a concept a lot of people have trouble with, and there is an
entire theory ("The Theory of Constraints") developed by Eliyahu M.
Goldratt, about it. Mr. Goldratt's book, *The Goal*, is one of the most important managerial works ever written, and though I don't hear *The Goal* ref-
erenced in other books on lean, The Theory of Constraints and the culture
of lean are closely connected.

To illustrate the Theory of Constraints, think of a pipe with water running
through it. If the pipe is uniform in size, a uniform amount of water will

be able to run through the pipe at all locations. Now imagine connecting a smaller pipe to the end and then running as much water through as the pipe will handle. The outflow will be reduced.

If many pipes of varying widths were connected, and the outflow was measured at different places in this series of pipes, the water flow would be even, even though many of the connected pipes would be capable of handling much more water than what would actually be running through them.

The narrowest pipe in the sequence will always be the one that determines the throughput of the entire series of pipes, and the narrowest pipe is the only pipe you should change to increase the flow. Changing other pipes would not help.

Improving the wrong part of one's Gemba is just like replacing the wrong pipe. Improving the wrong part of the Gemba will not improve the flow, whereas replacing the narrowest pipe will have a huge impact on the flow. The narrowest point is a bottleneck, and the pace water can run through that point determines the pace of the entire system.

A manufacturing process, or any process, will resemble that series of pipes, with some subprocesses being able to handle a larger flow than others. If a company tries to run its entire operation at 100% efficiency, that company will find that it cannot be done: some processes will have inventory piling up in front of them, and other processes will be starved for work. Those processes where inventory piles up are bottlenecks, and the biggest bottlenecks will tend to have the most piles of work in process inventory.

We tend to think of inventory as piles of material, but there are different types of inventory. Time, for example, can be a form of inventory, and particularly when we are talking about processes which take place outside a manufacturing plant. Data can be inventory. There are many types of inventory, but in all cases there is some kind of cost in carrying it.

I was a computer programmer when I was studying lean, and I began to wonder if the theory of constraints was applicable to computer code. The theory says anytime there is a series of dependent steps, if the output varies, constraints will exist. Computer programs are a series of dependent steps (lines of code), and the output certainly varies – hence the need to have code. I decided that computer code may fit in with the theory of constraints, and began to structure my code, not based on the number of lines I had to write, but on the number of lines that would have to execute. Initially, since I was not focusing on re-using code, I wrote more code, but after a while, I began to think of my code as akin to a manufacturing process, and structured my code into what I thought of as work centers. Pretty soon I was writing even less code than I had been when I was focusing on writing less code, and my code ran faster than it ever had before, with fewer bugs. I could not physically see the data within a running program, but it is there, it does represent a form of inventory, and it does bottleneck. Most programmers improve the speed of their programs by throwing more memory or more processing power at them. I found that I could also improve the performance of my programs by improving the data throughput – just like in a manufacturing center.

Once bottlenecks are identified, prioritize other functions around them. Anything feeding a bottleneck, that runs faster than the bottleneck, will create inventory. Slow those processes down, ideally by moving some of the people working these processes elsewhere. Processes downstream of the bottleneck may be starved for work, and if they are starved, they will already be running slower than they are capable of. Balance these with the bottleneck, ideally by moving employees away from these processes. You may be able to move employees to bottlenecks to improve the throughput of the bottlenecks, and since an improvement in a bottleneck improves the throughput of the whole organization, even small improvements are worthwhile.

The best example of a bottleneck I ever saw was in Marine Corps Advanced Combat Training. All Marines took this course after Boot Camp, and every Monday morning we would put packs on our backs and do a very long forced march, out to wherever we were training for the week. Our class commander was a marathon-runner. He would get up early, and run the course prior to the forced march. After running the course, he would put a big bladder of water on his back, and jog the course again, this time with our company in tow.

There was nothing even about these forced marches. Each Marine would start out at some pace, and all of a sudden the people in front of the Marine would take off at a sprint, forcing the Marine to sprint as fast as he could to catch up. Then the people in front of the Marine would come to almost a dead stop, having caught, and almost run over, the people in front of them. Then the people in front would sprint again. The whole march was conducted as a series of sprinting and stopping exercises, and it got worse as you moved further back from the front. At the back of the formation, it was absolutely brutal, and a formation that might ideally be a couple hundred yards long would stretch out for miles by the end of the march.

Mr. Goldratt, in *The Goal*, uses essentially the same example, with a boy scout troop marching through the woods. The "product" the line "produces" is the trail it consumes by traveling over it, and the length of the column represents work in process inventory. As the line gets longer, there is more inventory, making the process more expensive.

The reason the forced march gets so erratic is that there are little variations in pace all through the formation, and the effect of those variations compound further back in the formation, until at the end of the formation the variations are extreme.

Somewhere in the formation is the slowest Marine. This person cannot keep up with the people in front of him, and though there may be erratic running and stopping in front of the slowest Marine, things will be much worse behind him.

The front of the column will reach the finish line with the class commander, but the march is not finished until the last Marine makes it in, and that will be quite a bit later than the commander finishes with the front of the column.

We had a truck that followed the formation, picking up stragglers. In several forced marches more than a third of the company got picked up by the truck. The truck would fill, head to the training area (where the march was heading), drop off the Marines who had dropped out of the march, and then head back to pick up more Marines. The Marines who dropped out lost their weekend privileges, and if a Marine was toward the back of the formation at the start of the march, it was almost a forgone conclusion that he was going to drop out. In the back of the formation, entire platoons dropped out, just as at the back of a supply chain, entire businesses drop out.

In the fleet, most units put the slowest Marine at the front of the column to set the pace. Columns are much tighter when the slowest Marine sets the pace, and yet there is still some variation behind this Marine, causing Marines to run and stop, and causing the line to lengthen. It would not lengthen as much as in Advanced Combat Training, but it lengthens nonetheless. The reason is that there is still some variation in the pace of each Marine behind the slowest one, and that variation still compounds as the line moves further back from the front.

Mr. Goldratt suggests that the way to minimize the run/stop effect is to put the slowest person in the front, setting the pace, and to put the second slowest person behind them. The third slowest person goes next, and so on down the line, until you have the fastest person at the rear. There will still be some variation, but each person is faster than the person in front of them, and thus has no problem keeping up. Gaps close quickly, and the line stays much tighter.

PULL IS BETTER THAN PUSH

To get an operation to function as efficiently as possible, try to make it operate as if the bottleneck is at the end of the operation, and instead of pushing product into the bottleneck, have the bottleneck pull material when it needs it. Between lines, there should be just enough inventory to keep the bottleneck from running out of work. Operations that pull material are more efficient than operations that push material.

Balancing a production line is a lot like balancing a line of people marching. In both cases, you try to balance the line with the bottleneck, giving each process just enough excess capacity to catch up when variation occurs, such that the bottleneck always has a smooth flow of material going through it.

Some parts of an organization might have a special impact on how well the bottlenecks functions. If a computer crash shuts a bottleneck down, since the bottlenecks determine the pace of the entire operation, the entire operation might as well be shut down. It is imperative to keep bottlenecks running, and to do everything possible to increase the flow at bottlenecks, even if that means outsourcing and/or adding manual processes alongside the bottlenecks. Efficiency at the bottleneck is far less important than throughput.

One easy way to increase the capacity of a bottleneck is to run it 24×7 even if the rest of the company does not run 24×7.

As a company increases the flow of its bottlenecks and/or augments a bottlenecks' output, it may find that other things become bottlenecks. Bottlenecks move to new processes as existing bottlenecks are improved. Companies must always be on the lookout to see when bottlenecks move, and must always focus on the new bottlenecks as they emerge.

TO AUTOMATE, FIRST DO IT MANUALLY

Perhaps the most important note on automation is that a person cannot automate a process unless they first know how to do that process manually.[3] I've seen people try to automate processes they did not truly understand, and in all cases, before they get the automated process to work, they have to figure out the manual process. If someone is in charge of automating anything, whether that person is in IT, is a builder of robots, or whatever, utilize the Lean axiom of "go see" and learn how to do the process *manually* before trying to improve upon it. Keep in mind too that the people who perform a process every day already know how to do it. Utilize that knowledge by asking good questions to the people who perform the process being automated.

NOTES

1 *I May Be Wrong, But I Doubt It*, Douglas Hicks (self published), 2008
2 *The Goal*, Eliyahu Goldratt, North River Press, 1984
3 This is probably the root-cause behind the deadly crashes of the Boeing 737 Super Max. IT people, who were not pilots, and who did not know how to do the process manually (flying the airplane), programmed in a 'safety feature'. When the safety feature malfunctioned, the pilots did not have enough time to override it and save the aircraft. Ironically, the 'safety feature' killed people.

5

Maturing Markets

We have all seen engineers develop ideas for companies and then, for whatever reason, decide not to implement their ideas. Sometimes, the engineer then builds his own company.

Virtually all companies are founded in a similar way, even if the originating idea did not come from someone who was, technically speaking, an engineer.

At first, everything goes well. The company grows and prospers around this idea, causing hiring and expansion. Years go by, and the company has tens of millions of dollars in revenues, and though revenue growth may start to slow, there is still plenty of revenue, and the company continues to expand.

As revenue growth continues to slow, so too does profitability. The business owner knows the problem is not the product, for the product is the same as it was when the company was successful. The entrepreneur has even improved the product over the years. As years go by, however, the company begins struggling just to make monthly payroll, and though there may be many theories about what the problem is, the owner does not seem to have an answer, other than to tell employees that if they just did whatever the owner would do in any given circumstance, everything would be fine.

Actually, companies like this are only rarely as profitable as they could be even in the good years. The bad years that invariably follow come, not because the business has somehow changed in a negative way, but because the market changed, and the business did not.

BUSINESSES MUST CHANGE WITH THE MARKET

Markets mature. There is no way around that, and even if a company is not in a mature market today, eventually it will be. Understanding maturing markets, and knowing how to deal with them, is critical to the long-term success of any business. This needs to be a core competency of any business, no matter the size, or the market.

Sometimes the change required is radical; Walgreens started out as a restaurant chain before using its shrinking profitability in restaurants to fund a radical transformation into the convenience store/pharmacy industry. Usually, the change is less transformational than Walgreens, but markets do mature, and companies need to know how to handle it.

Both the core problem of maturing markets, as well as the base solution, are illustrated very clearly in two diagrams. The first is the Boston Consulting Group's *Product Maturation Quadrant Chart,*[1] shown below (Figure 5.1):

FIGURE 5.1
The Product Maturation Quadrant Chart

New products generally start as unproven technologies that may or may not successfully disrupt a market, and are in the question mark quadrant. Should the new technology prove itself, it will become a star for the company that developed it (or that was developed around it), making lots of money. Over time, other companies will adopt the same or similar technologies, and as market growth shrinks, the product will move into the cash-cow quadrant. If relative market share is low, the product begins to become unprofitable and falls into the dog category.

The key to this diagram is to understand that the same product can be in different quadrants for different companies. A product may be increasingly in the dog quadrant for some companies, while larger competitors may have efficiencies that keep the product in the cash cow quadrant.

Another chart gives some indication of a short-to-medium term solution for maturing markets: the *Process and Product Innovation and Industry Structure Chart*[2] (Figure 5.2):

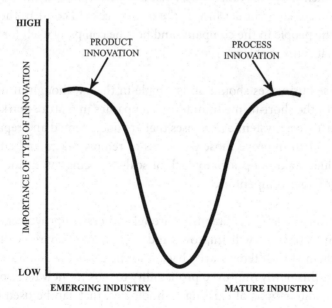

FIGURE 5.2
The Process and Product Innovation and Industry Structure Chart

This chart shows that as a technology matures, the ability to make that product more efficiently becomes more important than the ability to make incremental design improvements. *Process* innovation, then, becomes more important than *product* innovation. Essentially, product innovation creates new market segments, whereas process innovation squeezes more profitability out of existing market segments. Process innovation becomes more and more important as a technology matures.

The problem our hypothetical engineer-turned-entrepreneur has is this: being an engineer with little or no business knowledge, and being made to believe they know how to run a business by the good years when their product was a "star" or a "cash cow," the entrepreneur's skill set, centered around product innovation, becomes less and less important to the business' success. Most of the time, the entrepreneur is blind to their own deficiencies, and though they may hire others with the expertise they are lacking, they often won't make the changes they are advised to make; previous success mixed with industry knowledge making them believe that they know better.

One can spot these companies by watching the owner, who will reminisce about how great things used to be, and blame people when things go wrong (which they constantly do). Even key performers in the company will sometimes come under fire, as the owner seeks to confirm their bias that it is the people in the company, and not the company itself (or how it is run), that is the problem.

What these businesses should do is simple in theory, though difficult in practice. In the short-to-medium term, companies in mature market segments must create systemic processes that are documented and replicable. They must then improve those processes to remove waste and add customer value, making up for any lack of scale by being faster and leaner than their larger competitors.

As companies regrow profitability through process improvement, their competitive positions will improve, and their market shares will grow, moving them at least temporarily back into the cash cow quadrant. They should use this newly improved profitability to look for new technologies, and new combinations of existing technologies, that can be used to disrupt their industries, creating new market segments. They may also try to move into entirely new industries. This may require a combination of research and development, and strategic alliances with other firms.

The key difference between business people, and engineers, is that most engineers are trained to be product-oriented, whereas business people are trained to be market-oriented. Product engineers are usually the ones who form new companies, and they lack the training to see market changes, or to see the need for process improvement.

Note that neither product engineers, nor business people, are trained to be process-oriented. Business people are probably more so than product engineers, but really it is the industrial engineer, and/or the Deming disciple, who systemically looks at processes. Having a process person on staff can be of great assistance (as long as the business leadership is willing to listen).

Processes do not work if they are not followed, making actions that disrupt processes – no matter how important to the issues of the day – detrimental. That's not to say that each day's fires should burn out of control. Rather, *companies have to define new processes to deal with daily fires in ways that don't interfere with ongoing operations.*

FIRE FIGHTING: MAIN MISSION, OR SUPPORTING SUB-SYSTEM?

Think of a business for a moment as a city. Cities have fires that come up from time to time, but we do not see every citizen in the city grab a bucket and rush to the fire. If we did, then all activities in the city not related to putting out fires would cease every time there is a fire, and economic activity would come to a screeching halt. If a city only put out fires, then it would slowly be reduced to rubble, with each fire consuming another building, and nothing being rebuilt. Even if a city could both put out fires and rebuild burnt out buildings, unless it did more than that, it would cease to grow or prosper.

When one's business does nothing but chase each day's fires, it becomes like that city. It cannot respond to changing market conditions, changing customer needs, or changing circumstances. It is too busy responding to each day's fires, and as we all know, there can be a lot of fires. Someone in a company stuck in this sort of rut may even feel like the business is slowly turning into rubble.

Cities have fire departments that handle fires, so that everyone else in the city can continue to work on their day-to-day activities, and the city can grow. It probably does not make sense to have people sitting around in a business waiting for the next emergency to pop up, but the concept of having dedicated *systems* consisting of detailed *processes and procedures* for dealing with emergencies, to minimize the impact on the rest of the business, is relevant.

Perhaps even more important than having systems defined for dealing with day-to-day emergencies, is having processes and procedures setup to understand why emergencies occur, and particularly when they recur. Most "fires" are not unique circumstances at all, but are, rather, baked-into systems and processes. It is amazing, for example, how many critical emergencies sat on someone's desk for a long period of time, only to become "fires" when a deadline arrived. The chapter on Statistics Based Management can help one understand how to spot the difference between a real "fire" and a "fire" that is actually an undesirable part of a system. That chapter can help show how to handle both real fires, as well as things that feel like fires, but are really just a normal part of business operations. It is critically important to understand the difference, and to deal with each accordingly.

PRODUCT INNOVATION: TOP DOWN

The type of process improvements necessary to return companies in mature industries to a cash-cow state requires a cultural shift. The typical entrepreneurial culture is one where everyone in a company sits back and waits for the entrepreneur to step in and save the day. That's fine in a new market segment, where product innovation is what drives profitability. Product innovation occurs from the top-down (though see the section on marketing as it discusses how to know what innovations are necessary).

This is very different from process innovation, which occurs almost entirely from the bottom up. Process innovation requires a different kind of focus than does product innovation.

The need for product innovation does not go away. If anything the challenge to find new market segments always grows, but so too does the need to foster a culture that will allow a company to define, and improve, structured processes, so that they can continue to operate within existing markets profitably. Product innovation is important to start out in front, but it is process innovation that keeps a company there.

PROCESS INNOVATION: BOTTOM UP

A management team must be good at both product as well as process innovation, must understand which skill is relevant where, and must be able to use the correct kind of innovation at the correct time and place, and *also* to inspire others to do the same. To be a good manager at process innovation, one needs no knowledge of the industry or product at all, as process innovation is about asking the right questions of the right people, rather than coming up with the right answers. The knowledge a process person needs is in the people on the plant floor. The process person simply taps into that knowledge, and guides improvements the plant floor people will come up with themselves. It's a bottom-up process.

Product innovation is in many ways easier than process innovation, and yet it is an area where many companies still struggle.

I remember one company that made an ant spike to kill fire ants. The spike was made of brass, was very durable, and was several feet long. The idea was to shove the spike into a fire ant hill, and then to spray poison deep into the hill, where it would kill all the ants. My father had recently retired to Florida and had made a deal with a golf course, in which he would kill their fire ants, and in return, they would give him a free membership, letting him play as much golf as he wanted. Seeing an opportunity to help my father, I sent him an ant spike.

My father was initially very happy with the ant spike. It was solid and seemed to hold great promise. Having grown up in Michigan, my father knew very little about fire ants (as was also true of the engineer who had designed the spike), but he felt very comfortable with such a strong weapon for his newfound war. Unfortunately, the ant hills he used it on failed to die. It turns out that the way one kills a fire ant hill is to spray the outer surface of the mound, and let the worker ants bring the poison to the queen. When you spray the middle of the hill, you kill those ants in the part of the mound the poison hits, but they do not take the poison to the queen, and the hive survives. The ant spike did not work and was a total commercial failure (though my father's free golf continued). The moral of the story? Study the process before trying to improve it. Study of the fire ant feeding process would have led to the strategy of spraying the outer mound.

I can remember another company that had an abundance of fly ash, which is a waste product of coal. It turns out fly-ash can be turned into a plastic that looks like concrete. This company made plastic decorative shutters for houses, and thought that it would be great to have shutters for stucco houses. They began to make shutters out of fly ash, on the assumption that shutters that look like concrete would look better on stucco than do traditional plastic decorative shutters. Unfortunately, there are very few shutters on stucco houses. Making the shutters look like concrete failed to change that fact. The product was, like the ant spike, an abysmal failure.

NEEDS FIRST, SOLUTIONS SECOND

Both new products failed for the same reason: the companies in both cases were trying to generate demand for something they already had, without understanding the needs of people in the markets where they wanted to sell products. In other words, they took a solution and looked for a need, rather than taking a need and looking for a solution.

The ant spike, and concrete shutters, neither solved problems, nor fit into market demand. I can name a graveyard full of similar examples. More importantly, had the marketing research come before product development, a great deal of money that could have gone into other ideas might not have been wasted.

Product innovation is hard, as the section on marketing shows.

Process innovation is *also* hard, but for a different reason. The top of an organization does not really know what happens at the bottom of an organization, and the bottom of an organization does not really know what happens at the top of an organization. Most companies have a complete disconnect between the top and the bottom of their organizations. Furthermore, most people do what they have always done, or what they were trained to do, without regard for what is actually needed. As a wise person once observed: "If you do what you've always done, you'll get what you've always gotten."

I've met entrepreneurs who believed they knew everything that happened in their companies. That may have once been true for some of them, but as soon as that entrepreneur hired someone, they ceased knowing everything, and knowledge of what really happens where the rubber meets the road always shrinks as a business grows. It is impossible for the leader of a company of any size to even know what *should* happen everywhere, as they never know all of the details of each individual transaction. Loss of knowledge of what happens at the bottom of an organization is a byproduct of growth.

This can be illustrated very clearly by telling an organization that in one month's time it will cease making any reports unless specifically told by the person receiving a report how it is used. Furthermore, tell the people who receive reports that they have to circle the parts of the reports they actually look at, and that going forward only those parts will be created. Companies are often quite surprised to find out how many of their reports are not used at all, and how much time can be saved by not producing them. Companies are often even more shocked at how much better their reports become when they take only those parts that are actually used – usually less than 20% of what is produced – and put like items from disparate reports together into new reports, that are given to more people.

Both product and process innovation are always important. Process innovation makes it less costly to make higher quality products, and product innovation creates new products and services to open up new market segments.

THE FATHER OF PROCESS INNOVATION: HENRY FORD

Henry Ford is the modern father of process innovation, having created the production line, but Henry Ford's process innovations precluded product variation, or product change. Henry Ford's Process Innovations were changed radically by competitors (and later by Ford) to allow for product variation. Large batch sizes replaced single-piece flow, and mass-manufacturing replaced process efficiency. During and immediately after World War Two, there was seemingly limitless demand, which seemed to make process efficiency obsolete; what mattered were efficiencies of scale.

Toyota knew they did not have enough market share (at the time) to compete with Ford, Chrysler, and GM, using mass-manufacturing techniques, so Toyota went back to Henry Ford's original ideas, throwing away all of the changes the Big Three had made to them. They then applied W. Edwards Deming's ideas to Henry Ford's original production line, creating things like "quick changeover" to allow product variation, while still working toward one-piece flow.

TOYOTA: FEWER MISTAKES = LOWER COSTS

The result was that, though Toyota could not spread overhead costs across anywhere near as many units as could the Big Three, they could reduce overhead overall (dramatically), leaving far less overhead to spread out. They also found, as Deming had predicted, that a focus on single-piece flow, throughout the organization, helped to increase quality while decreasing costs. For their competitors, higher quality meant more inspectors, and an increase in costs. For Toyota, higher quality was achieved by reducing the opportunities to make mistakes, leading to lower costs.

The result was that Toyota was eventually able to produce a higher quality car at a lower price. This increased Toyota's market share, allowing them to spread what limited overhead they had out over a larger number of cars. Toyota achieved efficiencies of scale, even though that was never their goal.

In the meantime, Toyota led the industry in market research, finding out from customers what they wanted. Some customer requests were so simple that it blows the imagination anyone had to ask. How much, for example, did it cost to build a cup-holder? The built-in cup holder was not caused by some technological breakthrough (being just a divot in an arm rest), but by some consumer saying, "I love the styling and performance, but I have to hold my drink in my lap and it keeps spilling. Can't you give me some place to put my drink?"

Toyota sold millions of cars they would otherwise not have sold, simply because they built a cup holder into their cars before anyone else did.

Toyota also had improvements that required technological innovation, but those were also largely driven by talking to, and understanding, customers. Front-wheel drive was largely developed because customers did not like the way their cars slipped around in the winter in Northern states.

The idea to talk to and listen to one's customers (and more importantly, the end consumer) did not come from Toyota, but from Deming. Deming had a number of ideas, many of which are scattered throughout this book. Toyota did not originate, so much as *apply*, Deming's ideas.

Most of the radical new ways to run a business have already been developed by other people, like Deming, so when a company deals with process innovation, they are largely applying the ideas of others to their organization. That's not to say that it is impossible to come up with something entirely new (as did Henry Ford), but more likely companies will come up with variations on things already done, and improvements on the ideas of others.

Great companies do not choose between process and product innovation, but constantly strive to be leaders in both.

NOTES

1 Bruce Henderson, Boston Consulting Group, 1968.
2 "The Dynamics of Process-Product Life Cycles," Robert Hayes and Steven Wheelright, *Harvard Business Review*, March 1979.

6

One-Piece Flow, Inventory, and Rapid Changeover

One of the central tenets of lean manufacturing is the concept of one-piece flow, which is the notion that everything in one's organization should move through one piece at a time, arriving where it is needed when it is needed. In other words, everything "flows."

Henry Ford came as close as anyone to pure one-piece flow when he built the Model T on an assembly line. Ford, however, maintained his commitment to one-piece flow by doing everything possible to eliminate variation. Some variation was impossible to prevent, as the Model T was sold in touring models, truck models, and various other models designed for different purposes, but Ford was relentless in his pursuit of one-piece flow to the degree that in 1914, he told his engineers that henceforth the model T "will be offered in any color the customer wants, as long as it is black." The Model T changed over time, but only with incremental improvements, and those improvements then went into every car built. Options were minimized as much as possible.

At one point, Edsel Ford (Henry Ford's son) developed a V8 engine he hoped Ford could offer as an option to better compete with more powerful cars competitors were selling. Henry Ford sent Edsel to Europe for several months, and built an automated metal scrapping machine while Edsel was absent. When Edsel came back, Henry Ford took him to see the new automated metal scrapping machine, and to Edsel's horror, the very first thing thrown into it was his prototype V8 engine. Some say this indicates Henry Ford was against V8 engines, but really, he was against options, and he believed the four-cylinder engine already offered was overall the better choice. Sending the V8 into the scrap machine was his way of "teaching" his son that one-piece flow was more important than anything else.

General Motors utilized some of Ford's manufacturing techniques, but did not want to offer only one basic model of car, in only one color, with only one engine. General Motors wanted to have many models of very different cars with many options. Mass manufacturing using large batches was their solution.

Let me make a quick note on "manufacturing" that becomes more relevant in this chapter than in earlier ones, because too often we think of "manufacturing" in terms of products produced. In terms of lean, process rather than product is the key, and in that regard every one of us is in manufacturing of some kind. A programmer manufactures programs. A doctor manufactures improved health outcomes. A dentist manufactures better maintenance of teeth. Even a stay-at-home spouse manufactures a cleaner house, dinner, and children's activities. As such, when we talk about concepts related to manufacturing, they relate, in one way or another, to everything we do.

W. Edwards Deming was a quality guru who envisioned manufacturing as a scientific process, with improvements not only to the items being produced, but also to the process of manufacturing itself, utilizing the scientific method. Deming believed in statistical methods of control where, whenever a change was made, statistics could be used to determine whether or not the change was an improvement. Deming was laughed at in the United States, but the Japanese listened intently.

Taiichi Ohno was an engineer for Toyota who took Henry Ford's original ideas, threw out everything that mass manufacturing had added to it, and then took Deming's ideas and applied them to allow for variation. In doing so, Taiichi Ohno created the Toyota Production System, and became the father of what in America we call "Lean Manufacturing."

THE MOST AMERICAN OF GAMES: CATCHING UP

We Americans tend to be impatient, and so we generally do a very poor job implementing Lean. We Americans would rather play what Sean Connery said in the movie *Rising Sun*,[1] "is the most American of games: catching up." Most American companies that try to implement lean, try to implement the Toyota Production System, verbatim, rather than implementing the principles that led Toyota to create the Toyota Production System. In other words, we replicate specific processes that worked for Toyota with little regard for whether or not those processes will work for our companies, and then we call that "lean." Americans often copy lean tools without knowing when and why to use them.

Anyone who wants to do lean should study the Toyota Production System and should be capable of replicating the things Toyota does, but always with an eye for *why* Toyota does those things. Where the same kinds of problems Toyota overcame show up, using something akin to the same tools that worked for Toyota is generally a good starting point, but it is far more important that companies implement the ideas which led Toyota that develop those things, and that means going back to W. Edwards Deming. Lean is a culture and not a specific set of tools. If a company gets the culture right, the toolsets will follow.

LARGE BATCHES HIDE PROBLEMS

Taiichi Ohno took one-piece flow almost on a religious footing, and I would encourage everyone to do the same (I'll explain why toward the end of the chapter). Reducing batch sizes is not something to do only when hard savings from doing so can be found, but rather, batches should be reduced wherever possible. Ideally, batches are eliminated all together until everything is done one piece at a time. Companies do not want to reduce batch sizes in ways that make per-part costs higher, but companies should constantly look for ways to reduce batch sizes without incurring additional per-part costs, and should be willing to spend money to accomplish this. Large batches hide problems. Small batches expose those problems.

Companies can also drive improvements by reducing inventory levels arbitrarily – literally by finding where there are piles of inventory and making the piles smaller.

Inventory covers over problems, in the same way water can cover rocks and allow boats to sail past. Reducing inventory levels can expose those rocks, and once exposed, those rocks can be removed. Companies cannot fix problems unless they know they exist, so reducing inventory levels can be a useful tool in exposing problems.

American companies generally grade plant managers on how much uptime they have, with a goal of 100%. True lean companies do not want 100% uptime, as this much uptime means that no problems are being exposed, and thus problems are not being fixed. Reducing inventory levels may cause downtime, but that downtime is a low price to pay for the systemic improvements that can be made after the problems covered by inventory are exposed.

This does not mean that a company should go around and start removing all inventory everywhere it finds it, but it does mean that inventory levels should be systemically reduced, and that when problems occur that inventory was previously hiding, those problems should be solved, so that inventory is no longer needed to cover them up.

There are two ways to measure inventory. The obvious way is to go around and count it, but it is also worthwhile to tag raw materials coming in with the date and time received, and then as finished goods go out, to collect those tags and see how long different items tend to stay in a plant. A plant doesn't need to tag every piece of everything it receives, but it is nice to spot-check. As raw materials are consumed into different assemblies, the tags (which should say what raw component they were originally on) can be moved to the assembly. A great deal can be learned by looking at how long different materials stay in a plant, and the variability in how long different components are in the plant will tell even more.

THE IDEAL: PARTS SHOW UP JUST AS NEEDED FOR ASSEMBLY

Ideally, items are in a plant, on average, no more than *half as long* as it takes to build a finished good, with everything showing up only when needed. Items that are in a plant a lot longer than average should have a good reason for being around longer. If a company has some items that have a much longer stay than others, that company will want to know why, and will want to, if possible, take steps to reduce the length of time items stay. If a particular item has a great deal of variability, that likely means there is a large pile of inventory for that item somewhere, indicating that inventory is being used to cover up a problem. If inventory really is needed in that location, or where there are long lead times, consider making a first-in-first-out device to control the inventory level, and then reduce inventory to the bare minimum needed. Also, reduce lead times. Never assume that a supplier with a cheaper part but longer lead times is better than a supplier with more expensive parts and shorter lead times. In the long run, it may be better to take the shorter lead times, even if it costs a little more. It may also help to try to engineer production processes so that items with longer lead times are not needed until later in the production process.

Speaking of receiving items later in the production process, if a company can move the need for *expensive* components toward the end of the production process, it will help cash turns. That may be worthwhile to look at even if it means re-engineering processes and products. Anything a company can do to push the time it pays for materials out closer to (or even beyond) the time the company gets paid, will help cash turns, and improve profitability. But never sacrifice *quality* to do this!

One mistake I see a lot of small companies make is to use their suppliers as a bank. If a company has favorable terms with its suppliers, that's great. Use them. But some companies simply don't pay their suppliers when they are supposed to, using late payments as a form of borrowing. Whatever those companies may think they are saving, they are paying far more in fees, higher prices, and other costs related to negative business partnerships. It is OK to borrow to fund operations (and companies should do so until the cost of borrowing matches the profitability of producing more), but don't borrow from suppliers in violation of their terms. Borrow from a bank, sell bonds, or use some other legitimate source of lending.

One reason many companies need inventory is because they have processes using batches. Companies should do everything possible to reduce or eliminate the need for batch processing.

If a company has to use an oven, or some other piece of equipment that needs to hold onto parts for a period of time, the best such system is one where one part at a time is put in, and where parts go through on a conveyor, one at a time. As a compromise, small batches may be put in an oven with fixed process times (such as heat-treat). This can be timed so that one-piece flow continues both upstream, and downstream, of the oven, or other "fixed time" process machinery.

If a company has to use a press or some other piece of equipment that is difficult or expensive to change over, then start exploring rapid changeover techniques.

Most companies have a litany of reasons why rapid changeover won't work in their environment. It seems like rapid changeover is impossible in almost all environments until people implement it. Rapid changeover is one of those things that only works when people find ways to implement it, rather than reasons not to, and as with one-piece flow (which rapid changeover helps to build) I encourage people to take it somewhat on faith that it will help with more than just reducing inventory.

The truth is that there is no scenario where someone has not already figured out how to do rapid changeover. No environment is unique.

The ideal changeover time is the time it takes to process one part, which is referred to as "takt time" ("takt" being German for "pulse"), or "cycle time." Takt is calculated by taking the available production time and dividing it by the average customer demand in number of units. Takt will change when either of these numbers change.

Takt time is a critical measurement in any operation, and everyone should measure it. Companies should also work to reduce takt time, as described in the section on bottlenecks.

ONE-PIECE FLOW = FLEXIBILITY

As a company approaches one-piece flow, they will discover capabilities never before thought possible, such as the ability to produce closer to actual demand. Toyota can quite literally change vehicle models and colors in real time on their plant floor, allowing them to respond to real demand, producing cars in the exact models and colors needed by their dealerships. If we think about the complexities of needing the right components for, say a hatchback vs a sedan style car, with different option packages, and different colors, all on the same line running together – the right doors showing up in the right sequence at the right times, with all of the different components all being perfectly in sync, it really is quite impressive, and it provides Toyota with a tremendous competitive advantage.

Getting the kinds of capabilities Toyota has achieved requires the leap of faith I mentioned earlier (which stop being leaps of faith if you start using Activity Based Costing, as described in the chapter on Automation and Bottlenecks). All of the little steps along the way, where inventories are reduced and batches are eliminated, helps to create one-piece flow. It pays off far more than any of those incremental improvements made in isolation.

Not all companies are manufacturing companies, but these concepts still apply. Imagine a doctor's office where rapid changeover allows the right tests to be performed at the right place and time, so patients can go all the way from diagnosis through testing and treatment, all in one visit. Doctors could use takt times to reduce patient wait times. I've used these concepts not only on plant floors, but in IT departments (including in writing computer code), office environments – all over. Companies will find batches, inventory (including inventory of time or data), and changeovers happening all over the place. Companies need only look for opportunities, and opportunities will be found.

NOTE

1 *Rising Sun*, 20th Century Fox, 1993.

7

Statistics Based Management

W. Edwards Deming taught that 85% of all changes made by managers make things worse rather than better, and as crazy as that sounds, all someone has to do is to look at most organizations to see that this is just as true today, as it was in Deming's time (and I would venture government is even worse). The reason for this is two-fold. One is that managers rarely take the time to see and understand the systems and processes they are telling other people to change, and are thus making decisions without the base of knowledge needed to make *good* decisions. The other reason is that managers rarely measure the critical measurements needed to determine whether or not a change has had the desired effect.

If one thinks of the typical manager as someone who runs around screaming "YeeHAW" all day, while shooting a shotgun from the hip, with no apparent target in sight, that's not far from the truth.

I had a manger tell me once that he did not have time for statistics. This manager said that he "had his finger on the pulse of the organization" and had to "understand intuitively what was going on." The imagery he chose to illustrate his point was particularly telling about how wrong a statement this was – a doctor takes a pulse by counting heartbeats over the course of a minute; a pulse is a statistic.

Managers who do not take the time to measure critical measurements, and to use statistics to monitor changes, are not really managing, but are abdicating their roles as managers, and are likely making operations worse rather than better, as Deming warned.

In many small, entrepreneurial companies, the top manager (the owner/ founder) does not even know what their critical measurements are. It is amazing how many small manufacturing companies do not monitor such basic things as cycle times or quality levels. It is amazing how many production lines do not have key process indicators, based on things that commonly cause problems on the line. It is absolutely vital in any position for managers to know what things need to be measured, and then to measure those things.

The most basic tool for statistics-based management is the statistical process control chart. An example is shown below (Figure 7.1).

A control chart tracks some critical measurement, plotted over time, with an average, as well as upper and lower control limits. The control limits are three standard deviations from the average. It is not important that everyone in an organization know how to make a control chart, but everyone should know how to read them.

There are two kinds of variation, and the control chart allows us to differentiate between them. The first and most common kind is common cause variation. Common cause variation relates to normal, random fluctuations in process outcomes. The second kind of variation is special cause variation, which occurs when something that is not a normal part of a process happens. In a nutshell, anything that happens within the control

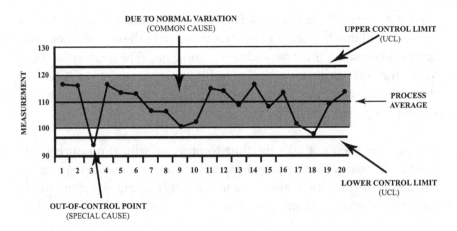

FIGURE 7.1
The Control Chart

limits can be assumed to be common cause variation, and anything that occurs outside of the control limits can be assumed to be special cause variation.

What managers often do is to measure a critical metric without control charts, and then confuse common cause and special cause variation; looking at individual plots as being indicative of positive or negative changes of some sort. Perhaps one order ships earlier than average, but within normal variation. The manager will say, "Boy – we sure did something good there! We need to find out what that was!" When a measure is worse than average, the manager will say, "Who screwed up?", and look for someone to blame. Managers may also notice that the better things get the more apt they are to get worse again, and that when things are generally going poorly they tend to get better. Since managers tend to give compliments when things go well, and tend to yell when things go poorly, managers may even begin to think that complimenting employees *makes* employees become complacent (and then things get worse) and that yelling at employees *makes* them work harder (and then things get better). The statistical term for what is really happening is somewhat self-explanatory. It is called "Regression to Mean."

When such scenarios occur, employees will say that they did the work exactly the same in both cases. Compliments and criticism for normal variation will drive employees crazy, teaching them to ignore the things managers say, for their own sanity.

Regression to mean is a simple concept: if a particular measurement is very close to a control limit, the chances are that the next measurement will be closer to the average. If managers look at control limits, and understand that anything within them is common cause variation that has nothing to do with employees performing "well" or "poorly," then they will recognize that those variations simply indicate what a process is *capable* of. Armed with this information, managers are suddenly in a good position to improve processes, and to handle special cause variation when it does, in fact, occur.

If multiple points on a control chart are outside of the control limits, then the process can be said to be "out of control," and the first thing a manager needs to do is to standardize the process, making it more consistent in operation so that the vast majority of points are inside the control limits. This is why lean advocates "standard work."

When fluctuations are all within the control limits, the process is acting "normally," and if "normally" is not good enough, then a manager will have to make changes to the process itself to improve the average, to reduce variability, and/or bring the control limits closer together. Yelling at people will not change the process – the process is a part of a system, and that system needs to be *structurally* changed to improve the output. In other words, the work needs to be done differently (and the changes made need to be tested to ensure that they truly improve the process).

It is possible for common cause variation to place a point outside of the control limits, but it is very rare (about a one in a million occurrence), so when a point occurs that is outside the control limits, special cause variation should be assumed. Under these circumstances, a manager should find out what happened that is outside of the norm and should take action to ensure that whatever it was, it does not happen again.

Things to look for that indicate special cause variation include the following:

1. Any point outside the control limits. Keep in mind that this can happen about one in a million times due to common cause variation.
2. Nine points in a row above or below the median. One could flip a coin every second for the rest of one's life, and the chances of landing on heads nine times in a row, or tails nine times in a row, is statistically nill. If you see the same thing in your processes, it is not random. If a process lands on one side of the median nine times in a row, something about that process is different than it was before. Ideally this occurs after a process change, and the plots are on the good side of the mean, indicating a statistically significant improvement! If a pattern develops where there are lots of points all above the mean, and then lots of points all below it, there are multiple processes in play, each with its own mean.
3. Six points in a row all increasing or all decreasing. Six points moving in the same direction in a row (it'll look like seven points as the first

point at the top or bottom of the series does not count) is statistically almost impossible. If one sees this, it indicates a special cause trend.

4. Fourteen points in a row alternating up and down. If one sees this, it indicates that variation is predictable rather than random. One should take steps to remove predictable variation.

5. Two out of three points in a row more than one sigma from the mean (on the same side). This indicates a small shift in a process, and may signify either something that is occasionally broken, or something that occasionally works better than expected, in a predictable way. If one can isolate the cause, one can either eliminate it, or replicate it, improving the process. Tool wear is an example of what can cause this kind of special-cause variation.

6. Four out of five points in a row within one sigma of the mean (on either side). This is another indication of a small shift in a process and can be interpreted the same way as point five, above.

7. Fifteen points in a row within one sigma of the mean. This pattern is called "stratification" and could be an indication that the process is less variable than it was before, or it could be an indication that one has multiple processes at play – something that changes periodically and then changes back. Either way this presents another opportunity to improve the process if one can isolate the cause.

8. Eight points in a row more than one sigma from the centerline is an indication of a mixture pattern, meaning that something in the process is pushing points away from the mean. Whatever that thing is, it probably needs to be corrected.

Note that not all special cause variation is "bad." There may be something specific about a process that makes special cause variation unavoidable. As an example, changes in humidity can affect textile spinning operations. Special cause variation is, however, something that should always be investigated and understood, as it often represents either a change in a process that had a statistically significant effect, or an opportunity to improve a process.

Common cause variation, on the other hand, indicates nothing more than that the process is working normally. A process working "normally" may not be working particularly well, but it is working within its normal range, and if that is not good enough, then the process itself needs to be improved.

When managers treat common cause variation as if it were special cause variation, such as by laying blame on people for doing "worse" than before, those managers are essentially running around with their hair on fire, setting other people ablaze. This is the most common, as well as the deadliest mistake managers make, as doing this creates new forms of variation in the process, making things worse rather than better.

This happens when employees respond to blame by trying to "fix" processes through process alterations. Deming called this "tampering with the process," and it increases variation, also making things worse rather than better. As a consequence, variation caused by bad management can be amplified even further by employees responding to that bad management.

Peter R. Scholtes describes this bad-manager effect in the book, *The Leader's Handbook,*[1] by describing a marksman who tries to improve his or her accuracy by adjusting his or her scope after every shot. After the first shot she is two inches to the left of the bullseye, so she adjusts her scope to the right. On the next shot she is an inch above the bullseye, so she adjusts her scope down an inch. Over time she makes lots of adjustments, and to her chagrin, her shot groups keep getting larger rather than tighter, meaning that she is becoming a worse shot than she was before.

The problem is that this marksman had some level of variation in his or her ability to shoot (common cause variation), and by adjusting the scope after each shot, all she was doing was adding those scope adjustments to the variation already in the process, compounding the variation. This is why in the Marine Corps, we shot three bullets to form a shot group, and then we made adjustments to move the center of the group. Really, the reason only three bullets are used is to save time and money; more bullets would be preferable. The goal is to create a shot *group* with a *center,* and then to move the center of the group onto the center of the bullseye.

Most managers are like the marksman, adjusting their scope after every shot. Rather than reducing variation, and making processes better, they increase variation, and make processes worse. Without statistics, they act emotionally, from an uninformed base, and make well-intentioned mistakes.

A manager who uses control charts to understand processes, or to "listen to the voice of the process," as Deming put it, is like the marksman who fires several shots to form a shot group, before adjusting their scope.

If a process is in control, and a manager makes a change, that manager should be able to track the change through critical measurements on statistical process control charts. If the change is positive, then one or more measurements should change in a positive way, causing special cause variation. The average may shift, the control limits may come closer together, or something else may happen indicative of a positive change. If a change is negative, then the average may shift in a bad way, or the control limits may go further apart. By making changes and then measuring the results, managers can see if changes are positive or negative, and can keep the positive changes, while rolling back the negative ones.

Control limits can also tell whether or not a process is capable of creating the results needed. If the control limits are outside of the customer's specifications, the process is not capable of meeting the customer's requirements consistently, and if the process is not improved, there will be trouble. Say, for example, a company is making a cap for a pill box, and the cap needs to have a one-centimeter lip, with a tolerance of 1.5 millimeters. If the upper and lower control limits are at 2 millimeters, then the process is not capable of keeping within a 1.5-millimeter tolerance, and caps with too big or too small of a lip will be common. If, on the other hand, the process has upper and lower control limits that are 1.3 millimeters, then as long as the process does not change, there is nothing to worry about with regards to that particular measurement. When control limits are well within specifications, a company may even be able to reduce costs while staying within control limits.

Everyone should teach their employees to read control charts. Employees do not all need to know what to take from all eight of the different indicators of special cause variation, but they should know when special cause variation occurs, so that they can call a manager. Employees don't need to know what drives the upper and lower control limits, but they should be able to tell when these things have shifted. Not only will employees be able to get a manager when they see something change in a statistically significant way, but employees will suddenly feel empowered, and will want to take an active role in helping to improve processes. Believe it or not, but employees who can read control charts discuss them, and enjoy experimenting with processes to try and improve them.

SIX SIGMA TAKES LONGER THAN LEAN

Many people think of Six Sigma when they think of statistics. Indeed, the above part of this chapter is very similar to Six Sigma. As a practitioner of Lean, I cannot recommend Six Sigma. The goal is to use Six Sigma methodologies (which are based on W. Edwards Deming methodologies), without being hand-cuffed into a rigid set of time-consuming, and non-value-adding, rules. Six Sigma is a quality tool for people who do not understand statistics. Six Sigma takes longer than simple, good decision making, based on a firm understanding of measured processes, as taught by Deming.

What Six Sigma is good at, is helping an entire company use statistics in their decision making. To do that with Six Sigma, however, everyone needs to learn Six Sigma – the teaching of which is a time consuming and expensive undertaking. It is easier to teach people how to make and interpret control charts, and to show them how (and where) to use them.

Statistics based management is nothing more than the application of the Scientific Method to management. One starts with a hypothesis, in which one says, essentially, "If I change this, the process will improve based on these measurements." One then makes the change and looks at the measurements to see if the hypothesis holds. One also looks at other measurements to ensure there are no unintended consequences. Finally, if the change is statistically positive, one makes it a part of the improved process, and it becomes the new standard work. If the change cannot be shown to be positive, one rolls it back.

The process of standardizing, and then improving processes, is detailed in the next chapter.

Keep in mind that there are processes at various levels of an organization, including at the top. There are a number of books, such as *Learning To See*,[2] by Mike Rother and Mike Shook, that illustrate the best way, in my opinion, to map-out and understand organizations. These books teach not only where and how value is added, but also where value is not added and where waste can be removed. The process detailed in that book ("Value Stream Mapping") is invaluable, and if undertaken, I recommend starting at the top of the organization, asking what the true value stream of the whole is, and then working down from there, department by department, and system by system, until value-stream maps have been created for each part of the organization, and then tied back into the company-wide value-stream. On each value stream, think about what can be measured to help ensure that the process is producing maximum value, with minimal waste.

This is in many ways the most important chapter of this book, as many of the other chapters assume statistical tools are in place, and that changes in processes are being verified against them.

NOTES

1 *The Leader's Handbook*, Peter Scholtes, McGraw-Hill, 1998.
2 *Learning to See*, Mike Rother and John Shook, The Lean Enterprise Institute Inc., 2003.

8

Standardized Operations and Process Improvement

Improving company operations through systemization and standardization should become a core competency of any organization. This involves creating documented "best practices" employees are expected to adopt, and then working with employees to constantly improve those "best practices." One should work to build an organization that learns and improves over time. This is the type of organization that can grow profitability faster than the natural erosion inherent in maturing markets (see Chapter 5 on Maturing Markets). Even if a market is not mature yet, reducing waste, and focusing on value-adding activities can always enhance the bottom line.

Employees can be resistant to this kind of standardization, and standardized processes tend to slip back to non-standard operations if standards are not enforced. Because of this, standardizing processes does not work without the total support of the entire management team. Companies that successfully standardize (and make the other cultural changes discussed in this book) generally lose around 1/3 of their workforce, and some of the people who leave are invariably people companies do not want to let go. Companies must be willing to let go those who are not onboard with standardization. Companies must also be willing to fire with cause any employees who work against what will become the new cultural norms.

Standardized operations are operations that are done the same way, every time, regardless of who is doing them. Once operations are standardized, they can be improved upon, particularly if critical measurements (see the chapter on Statistics Based Management) exist to measure changes against.

Many question the level to which operations must be standardized. Frankly, it depends on the operation. On a manufacturing floor, line workers can standardize what they do to a very granular level. Small things like turning the wrist 45 degrees after grasping a tool, can make a difference in cycle times, quality, the comfort and safety of the worker, and a host of other issues. In other parts of the company, such as in the office, natural variance may make it more difficult to standardize to the same degree as on the plant floor, but it can be done.

Luckily, the quality and granularity of standards can be improved over time. Workers should, in fact, be encouraged to constantly look at standards and ask how they can be improved, and there should be rewards for those who come up with changes that show measurable improvements.

STANDARDIZING ... COOKING BURGERS?

My first job was at McDonalds, when I was sixteen. I worked in the grill area. McDonalds had, at the time, very rigid standards defined to what seemed like (to a sixteen-year old) an incredibly granular level, and though I may not remember them exactly, making "regulars" (hamburgers and cheeseburgers) consisted of steps similar to the following:

1. Place the buns for up to 12 regulars upside down on a bun-tray.
2. Slide the bun tray into the toaster.
3. Place a bun spatula into the buns where they are separated (top from bottom) and separate the tops from the bottoms.
4. Pull out the bun spatula with the bottoms on them and place the spatula on top of the toaster.
5. Close the toaster.
6. Grasp up to six frozen hamburger patties in each hand.
7. Place the patties in rows of six, from the front of the grill toward the back, and hit the grill timer.
8. When the grill timer beeps the first time, sear the patties.
9. When the bun toaster buzzes, remove the bun tops and place the bottoms in the top part of the toaster.

10. The grill timer should beep again. Flip the patties with the patty spatula.
11. Dress the buns in the following order:
    a. One-shot mustard (special machine provided)
    b. One-shot ketchup (special machine provided)
    c. One pinch of onions
    d. One pickle slice
    e. Call out to manager "Cheese on <number> regs please"
    f. The manager will say, "On <number> regs go <number> thank you"
    g. Repeat: "On <number> regs go <number> thank you"
    h. Place cheese on the number of regs specified to have cheese.
12. When the grill timer goes off, pull the patties two at a time and place them on the buns.
13. Pull the bun bottoms out of the toaster with the bun spatula.
14. Place the bun spatula with the bun bottoms directly over the tray of regs.
15. Holding the buns in place at the back of the bun spatula with one hand, slide the bun spatula out from under the bun bottoms so the bun bottoms land on the buns.
16. Place the regs on top of the grill and push them toward the front.
17. Say "<Number> regs up please."
18. The manager will repeat, "<Number> regs up, thank you."

The ketchup, pickles, onions, and other ingredients were always stored in exactly the same place on the staging table, and were as accessible as possible whenever they were needed (Figure 8.1). The mustard and ketchup guns had to be held in a specific way, and we were supposed to come to a complete stop over each bun when we shot mustard and ketchup. Each one of the 18 steps had a specific way we were trained to do them. There was even a specific height we were supposed to hold the ketchup and mustard dispensers over the buns when dispensing condiments.

Keeping things clean, and placing the things that are most needed, closest to the work area, is called "5S" in lean parlance. 5S stands for "Sort," "Set in Order," "Shine," "Standardize," and "Sustain," and relates to setting up work areas so that they are organized and tidy, with a specific place for everything. Items that are only rarely used are moved out of the work area.

FIGURE 8.1
The Burger Flipper

I learned to cheat. I found that if I did not stop the mustard gun, and moved it at just the right speed, while my mustard might be in slight lines on the bun instead of in one clump, it was still all in the central part of the bun, and I could shoot the mustard faster. I created tricks with the ketchup, with the spatula, with the onions and pickles – with every aspect of my job to do it faster than before. Eventually I was fast enough dressing buns that I could put the meat down *before* putting the buns in the toaster, and still have enough time to dress the buns before the meat was done. This reduced the cycle time of the entire operation. I became easily the fastest grill person in the store, or for that matter, in any store I worked in. When there was a rush and we were shorthanded, every manager wanted me in the busiest spot, knowing that no matter how busy it got, they would not wait for whatever food I was cooking.

I did not follow the McDonalds standards. Rather, I continuously worked to improve them. I treated everything as a race, and if I was not racing other people, I was racing myself.

HOW TO MAKE THE WORK FUN: COMPETE AGAINST A STANDARD

Some of the other employees thought I was crazy. Why work so hard for minimum wage ($3.35 an hour at the time – about $6.70 an hour today if adjusted for inflation), they would ask me. The answer was that an eight-hour shift took a long time in the grill area, and by busting my butt to be as fast as I could possibly be, I made the time pass faster. I was making a mundane job fun by competing against myself.

I hadn't had any training at the time in lean manufacturing, but the standardization of the grill area was fascinating, as was the notion that I could improve upon those standards. I had the right attitude. My attitude was contagious to *some* other employees (who also took pride in becoming faster), and my attitude made an otherwise mundane job fun. The store manager was supportive, and over time I became more and more of a leader in the grill area. I also made very good friends – some of whom were almost as fast as I was – and the entire culture of the store reflected our efforts.

Really, the credit should go to the store manager, and some of the other managers of that McDonalds. They ran a tight shop, and allowed their employees to shine. I was not anything special. I was just an employee allowed by management to self-motivate.

In an ideal lean company, my improvements would have become the new standard, and all other employees would have been taught to follow the new standard.

The mundane jobs at any company can be fun if employees feel empowered to standardize and improve processes, and the more employees do improve, the stronger the culture of the organization becomes.

Managers, however, do not standardize operations. Managers only guide and instruct employees on standardizing operations. Those who perform each role (the workers) are the best ones to standardize and improve what they do. The management team must work with all employees to, over time, standardize and document everything. Companies should strive for QS9000 levels of process documentation without the loss of improvability QS9000 and similar programs entail. In other words, companies want standards they can continue to improve.

When standardizing operations, don't forget to standardize cycle times (the time from starting one operation on one unit to starting that same operation on the next unit) based on the flow of the entire value stream, as measured at bottleneck processes. It makes no sense to have some processes starved for work and other processes working to make things faster than they can be started on by the next process in line.

Build consensus from the people who perform a task on which method is the best, based on factual evidence. There will obviously be some variation in actual processing time (versus takt time) if a process allows everyone to go at full speed, and there will be some variation in how long it takes different people to do a process, even on a production line where the takt time is not variable (since takt is based on customer demand). Whatever the takt time needs to be to meet the customer demand rate, workers need to be able to consistently perform all tasks within that time (with training), and need to be able to do so while producing quality output. A longer takt time that is consistent is better than a shorter takt time that can't be consistently maintained.

Remember, *takt time is calculated as the available production time divided by the number of units required to meet customer demand*. If the available production time is 8 hours a day (480 minutes) and we divide by a customer demand rate of 80 units a day, then takt time = 6 minutes. A new unit should be produced every 6 minutes to fulfill customer orders. But what if the processing time (the time it takes to build one unit) is more than 6 minutes? The customer demand rate per day cannot be changed, so it might be necessary to add a night shift to increase available production time. By adding the night shift, the company increases the numerator (to more than 480 minutes available production time), which is divided by the same denominator (80 units a day ordered by customers). The takt time is longer, and suddenly the process is capable of meeting the demand.

Here is an example: if customer demand for eyeglass frames was 80 per day, and a single worker worked an 8-hour shift, then available production time (8 hours × 60 minutes) = 480 minutes. 480 minutes available production time divided by 80 frames = 6 minutes takt time. One eyeglass frame must be produced every 6 minutes in order to meet customer demand.

Now suppose the lone operator's actual processing time was 8 minutes to complete each frame. 480 minutes available production divided by 8 minutes processing time = 60 frames produced per day. This is 20 frames short of the actual customer orders of 80 frames a day. The company must take action, or it will start losing sales.

Some options:
  a. Study the process (perhaps with a value stream map) and find ways of improving the process so that one operator can complete a frame in 6 minutes instead of 8 (while still maintaining the quality of the frame, of course). This will meet customer demand, as the cycle time of 6 minutes matches the takt time of 6 minutes.
  b. Add 160 minutes to the existing 480 minutes of production time by hiring a part-time worker to work 160 minutes a day. 480 + 160 = 640 minutes of production time available daily. 640 minutes divided by customer demand of 80 frames a day = 8. With the additional minutes of production time available, the new takt time is 8 minutes. The new takt time of 8 minutes matches the processing time of 8 minutes daily customer demand can be met.[1]
  c. Do both. Adding production time may buy time to perform a process study and test some possible process improvements that could reduce processing time.

DISTRIBUTE OPERATOR TASKS ON A PRODUCTION LINE SO ALL CAN BE DONE WITHIN TAKT TIME

Balance processes as much as possible by adding tasks to some work stations, and taking steps away from other work stations, to make each standardized procedure come as close to the takt time (without going over) as possible. I don't mean making up tasks – I mean taking tasks from one position and giving them to another. Do not forget to consult the people whose processes are being changed when deciding what changes to make. If possible, it is better to involve them in making changes than to dictate the changes to them. Having someone with some industrial engineering experience can be helpful. Industrial engineering is incredibly underrated in today's business world.

There can be a correlation between speed and quality, in which, if a process is pressed to go too fast, quality suffers. No process should be pressed to go so fast that quality suffers. If a worker hurries, it can also lead to safety accidents.

Companies need to measure the performance of their processes so that they know whether or not each change really is an improvement. Measure whatever the critical measurements should be, and remember that it is not always related just to quality and takt time.

There are various ways to document processes. I find that flow charts and process charts work best. Ideally they should be clearly visible where the process is performed. Utilize 5S: things used the most frequently need to be the most conveniently accessible, with things that are used less frequently being further away and less accessible. Everything should have a specific place, and every work area should be kept spotless. See the manual, *5S Made Easy,*[2] by David Visco, of the5sstore.com.

Do not subscribe to QS 9000 or any similar quality/standardization standard. Peter Scholtes, in his book, *The Leader's Handbook,*[3] prints a letter by Arthur Wellesley, the First Duke of Wellington, that describes bureaucratic standardization to a tee:

Gentlemen:

Whilst marching from Portugal to a position which commands the approach to Madrid and the French forces, my officers have been diligently complying with your requests, which have been sent by H.M. ship from London to Lisbon and thence by dispatch rider to our headquarters.

We have enumerated our saddles, bridles, tents and tent poles, and all manner of sundry items for which His Majesty's Government holds me accountable. I have dispatched reports on the character, wit, and spleen of every officer. Each item and every farthing has been accounted for, with two regrettable exceptions for which I beg your indulgence.

Unfortunately the sum of one shilling and ninepence remains unaccounted for in one infantry battalion's petty cash, and there has been a hideous confusion as to the number of jars of raspberry jam issued to one cavalry regiment during a sandstorm in western Spain. This reprehensible carelessness may be related to the pressure of circumstances, since we are at war with France, a fact which may come as a bit of a surprise to you gentlemen at Whitehall.

This brings me to my present purpose, which is to request elucidation of my instructions from His Majesty's Government, so that I may better understand why I am dragging an army over these barren plains. I construe that perforce it must be one of two alternative duties, as given below. I shall pursue either one with my best ability, but I cannot do both.

1. Train an army of uniformed British clerks in Spain for the benefit of the accountants and copy-boys in London, or perchance
2. To see to it that the forces of Napoleon are driven out of Spain.

Your most obedient servant,

Wellington

What Sir Arthur Wellesley was referring to, in a very humorous way, and what Peter Scholtes was also illustrating, is the need for standardization efforts to serve a larger purpose. As Wellington's letter shows, it is possible to measure many trivial things. One must ask, "will this measurement help us give the customer what the customer wants?" If the answer is "no," drop the measurement (unless it is a regulatory requirement from government). Companies should not standardize just to wave a flag outside the office with "QS 9000 Certified," or some other such thing on it. When I see

"QS9000" waving proudly outside an office, I equate it with a white flag of surrender, the plant having surrendered its freedom to improve.

Processes should be standardized to get everyone in their organization to do everything the best way known (note I did not say the best way *possible*). Then, companies can improve continuously, upon the best way known.

When standardizing and improving support roles, always keep in mind how support roles interact with, and affect, the company value stream. It is very easy, particularly with support roles, to maximize support department efficiencies that end up coming at the expense of the rest of the organization. In systems theory, this is called "sub-optimization." That isn't to say one should not standardize support roles – ideally everything becomes standardized. It is always critical, however, to standardize processes so they benefit the *overall* organization's value stream, even if doing so comes at the expense of local efficiencies. Never allow a support role to hinder the Gemba!

As an IT person, I really struggled with standardization. My job was different every day. The problems I faced changed daily. Some days I was programming. Some days I was observing processes with an eye toward automating them. Some days I was troubleshooting something broken – a server, a network issue, or whatever. The question I had was what there was to standardize when I had no standard output and no standard tasks.

The answer was methodologies.

STANDARDIZING METHODOLOGIES GIVES LEVERAGE OVER RESULTS

I can standardize how I troubleshoot problems. That's actually really easy and effective to do: I strove to always cut the potential issues in half. I would separate a problem between hardware and software, between a computer or the network, between programming and data. Each time I ruled out 50% of the possible root causes, I also narrowed down much closer to the actual root cause.

I can standardize components. Should I buy Western Digital or Seagate hard drives? If I measure how long they last, and what kind of failure rates I get on both, I can determine which is more reliable (and can see when the reliability changes).

I can standardize how I program. There are lots of different standards for how to program and how to structure code. I came up with my own style of programming, which I called "Lean Programming."

Depending on the role looked at, it may be possible to standardize the information gathered in a phone call, or given as output on a sales sheet.

THE REAL GOAL: IMPROVEMENT OF PROCESSES

Standardization is the only springboard to the real goal: *improvement of processes*. Standardization is important only because processes cannot be improved unless they are done the same way every time.

Because standardization is a prerequisite to improvement, it is vital that standardization not occur in ways that preclude improvement, or that act as a barrier to improving, such as by subscribing to QS 9000 or similar programs.

Under the Automation section, we touched on process improvement by saying that even when we automate, the goal is not "automation" but "process improvement," and we said that it is very possible to automate a process in a way that is not an improvement. We discussed many of the pitfalls automation can cause. It is necessary to stress again that while automation can be a part of improving a process, automation and process improvement are not the same thing.

"Automation" simply means taking a process that involves people and making it either involve fewer people, or making it involve no people, through the application of machines and/or computers. "Process improvement" involves taking a process and making it better in a measurable way, without causing problems elsewhere. It is entirely possible to automate a bad process. Use automation as a reason to take a fresh look at processes, and improve them before automating. Improvements may make automation unnecessary.

TRADE-OFFS VS. IMPROVEMENTS

If an improvement in one or more metric causes other metrics to get worse, that is not an improvement, but is, rather, a trade-off. Many companies approach quality as a trade-off with price (higher quality costing more to achieve). Under this view, whether a quality improvement is positive or negative is based on the market segment the company is trying to meet, and on how well the company already meets that market segment. Generally speaking, if a change leads to higher profitability, then the trade-off can be said to be an improvement for the company. Higher profits finance future product improvements.

Ideally, cost and quality both improve. The section on Quality discusses how to improve both measures at the same time.

There are improvements that do not relate directly to cost or quality. Reducing batch sizes, decreasing takt times, balancing one's processes to the flow of bottlenecks, creating one-piece flow throughout an organization (as much as possible), reducing the need for inventory, increasing change-over speed (ideally to no more than the takt time), and various other activities are also improvements. Even if they do not improve quality, or reduce costs immediately, over time they will.

Most companies look at improvements with a one-off view, where each improvement has a set, measurable benefit. Some improvements, and particularly those outside the Gemba, really are like that, but smart companies focus first and foremost on process improvements that can over time completely change the capabilities of their businesses.

Rapid change-over can change the capabilities of a business. If a company reduces inventory enough, it can change the capabilities of the business. Reducing batch sizes (ideally down to one-piece flow) can change the capabilities of a business. Making every employee a quality manager can change the capabilities of a business.

VALUE STREAM MAPPING: A MAP OF HOW YOU DO WHAT YOU DO

There are methodologies that can help spark process improvements, and they invariably revolve around a chart known as a Value Stream Map. I mentioned Value Stream Maps (and the book *Learning To See*) briefly in the section on Statistics Based Management, and I talk about Kaizen Events in the section on Strategic Decision Making. These two things work very well together.

If a company has someone on staff who knows how to do Value Stream Mapping (they can hire someone or have someone trained if they do not), then they can use Value Stream Mapping in Kaizen events to help determine where improvements may be necessary, as well as what improvements to make.

A Value Stream Map is a form of flow-chart designed to show a process in terms of the value provided, and the time and inventory necessary to achieve that value. A process is broken up into a series of sub-processes, and the inventory and time taken for each process is designated.

Include the people who perform the process being improved whenever a kaizen event is held, as well as anyone in a customer or supplier role to that process. Also include some people who have nothing to do with the process itself, as they may be able to offer some fresh perspectives that people directly involved in the process won't think of. Start the event by drawing up a giant Value Stream Map, based on input from the participants, to show how the process currently operates. Once the value stream map, representing the "current state," is up on the wall, the people in the event will be able to see very obvious ways to improve the process. Discuss each step in the process, and whether or not it adds value, and then begin to draw a new Value Stream Map designating what the process might look like under ideal conditions, with as few non-value-adding steps as possible. If the team can implement that ideal state, begin designating the tasks necessary to do so, and then migrate to it. The new map becomes the new process. If the company cannot get to the ideal state immediately, draw an improved Value Stream Map as an intermediary, and use this as a precursor for more improvement projects to get ever closer to the "ideal state."

I hate the phrase "ideal state," as no state is ever "ideal." Other processes change, so even if one could make some process "ideal," it would stay that way for only a short time, and then it would be something that could be improved upon again. The word "ideal state" is used a lot in lean circles, so I use it too, but keep in mind that nothing is ever "ideal." Some use the phrase "future state."

To decide where to have kaizen events, it may help to bring in all of the top executives (along with anyone else who might be considered necessary or beneficial), and then to draw the whole company as a Value Stream Map, in a kind of a 35,000 foot view of the company's overall operations. This will illustrate obvious areas where improvement is possible, and the company can then call for kaizen events where improvement opportunities are found.

We did a company-wide Value Stream Map in the induction heating company I worked for. We found that the worst piece of the company's Value Stream was sales. There was no real "sales process," which led to erratic (and low) sales levels, and we found that the information from the sales team, which was then used by Engineering to design the induction heating equipment, was insufficient. Engineering documents then went to the production floor, where they were heavily modified – often by having the owner (who was also the primary sales person – really the only sales person who ever sold anything, though there were other sales people who sold nothing) blow up the design, with changes necessary to meet customer requirements the owner had never previously bothered to tell anyone about. These became "red-line" changes in the engineering documents. In truth, much of the engineering was done on the fly, on the plant floor, by the plant manager.

We also found that whenever a new job came up, the sales person would say, "This job is like another job we did in the past," and then the previous job was pulled back out and modified for the current job.

We found a number of problems. One was the lack of a sales process and thus a lack of sales (not paying sales people based on commission might have had something to do with that). Another problem was that the customer requirements were poorly communicated (if communicated at all) to the engineers, causing the engineers to design equipment without taking into account all of the customer's needs – and causing the owner (the only one who generally knew what the customer really wanted) to blow-up builds on the floor, with all kinds of changes, and expensive rework. Furthermore, the redline changes made on the floor were not documented, so when a similar job came up in the future, whatever problems had occurred before reoccurred. We also found that the sales team priced jobs based on whatever it took to close them, with little regard for what the job might cost, and that the delivery schedule was whatever the customer asked for, with no regard for what the company might actually be capable of delivering.

The purpose of this Kaizen event was not to fix anything, but to outline problems that needed to be fixed, and to identify what parts of the company needed further Kaizen events. There were obvious areas where improvements were possible (and not just in sales), and we had other Kaizen events for each of those areas.

Unfortunately, the most important member of the executive team was the owner, and he did not attend any of the Kaizen events. Nor did he always endorse the changes which came out of Kaizen events. We were able to make some significant improvements in a number of important metrics (and our customers noticed), but without the owner's support, we were not able to make cultural changes, and we only scratched the surface of what was possible.

One of the reasons I was not able to gain the respect of the owner was because I knew nothing about induction heating. There was, however, a tremendous amount of induction heating knowledge throughout the company, so I did not *need* to know much about induction heating. I only needed to provide good questions to those who knew induction heating, to listen to what I was told, and to diagram accurately what I heard. Often the owner acted as if I was creating process changes myself, and since I did not have the knowledge necessary to do that, he looked at those changes with suspicion and scorn. Had he attended our Kaizen events, he would have seen that I was only *leading* the change efforts. The changes themselves were created by the people who worked the processes being changed, and *they* had all the knowledge in the world.

This story is important for two reasons. One is that it illustrates Kaizen events with Value Stream Mapping, and the other is that it illustrates that the company culture is the most important part of the process. Without the right culture, process improvements will not last.

Another interesting side note is that kaizen events are almost by definition non-political. With everyone involved in a process, all together in the same room, the truth about the process invariably comes out. Even where people do not want change, the kaizen event itself works – the politics and resistance come afterward, when the company tries to enforce the new value stream map.

I was only involved in one Kaizen event that totally failed. It was the first one I ever attended. The company I worked for had hired a lean guru to help the company "go lean," and I was asked to join as someone who was totally unrelated to the process being looked at. The lean guru worked with the people whose process was to be improved, and we drew up a value-stream map. Some of the waste in the process was so obvious that even I could see it, and at this point in my career I knew nothing about value-stream mapping, and nothing about the process being looked at (except what had been drawn up on the value-stream map). The lean guru asked the group, "What might an ideal-state start to look like?," and immediately, all of the people who were a part of the process decided that the current state was also the ideal state. This occurred right after a company-wide layoff, illustrating why layoffs are counter-productive. Nobody in that room was going to work to improve the process right after having seen coworkers laid off, no matter how obvious the waste was... In their minds, process improvement = layoffs, and they did not want to be laid off.

If the leadership of an organization sounds like the owner of the induction heating company I worked for, then the leadership will have to change before significant improvements can take place. One can make incremental improvements without the support of the company leadership, but those improvements will be partial and temporary. Improvements should build upon each other like a snowball rolling downhill, and a company won't get there if those who are resistant to change have powerful executives to hide behind. Managers can't fire owners, but if there are leaders who are not onboard and who *can* be fired, fire them. Do not procrastinate. Fire them now.

NOTES

1 These calculations are based on perfect conditions which rarely exist in the real world. As noted above, there will be some variation in actual processing time. To allow for this, many factories aim for a processing time equal to approximately 80% of takt time. This allows for some "wiggle-room" to make takt and deliver to the customer on time.
2 *5S Made Easy*, David Visco, Productivity Press, 2015.
3 *The Leader's Handbook*, Peter Scholtes, McGraw-Hill, 1998.

9

Quality

Most companies view quality in terms of defects. If the defect rate is low enough (ideally down to a Six Sigma level of 3.4 defects per million) then they believe they have a quality operation. There is some truth to this, because if there are too many defects, a process cannot be said to be running at a high rate of quality. However, measuring quality strictly by defect rate is such a narrow view that it largely misses the point.

If a company does not have the market share to enjoy the same economies of scale larger competitors have, it must focus on the efficiency of each individual build, by doing *everything* right the *first time*. This is only possible if quality becomes the highest priority, bred-in at every level of the organization. Each employee must take pride in the quality of their work, and must learn to judge the quality of their work from the eyes of whomever or whatever uses their output. Each employee must also be a "quality engineer," with the power to correct those whose output they utilize.

Most employees, in most companies, gauge their jobs based on what they have always done in the past, on the assumption that if they keep doing what they have always done, then they will have performed quality work. This mindset ensures that the quality of the organization does not change, which also means that quality of the product or service cannot improve. If improvement is the goal, then this mindset must change; each employee must understand that if the person *receiving* their work is not happy with what is received, then quality work has *not* been performed, *even if there are no defects.*

What is true of the individual is also true of the organization, and most organizations rely too much on assumptions. Companies do not always take the time to find out what their customers really want, and thus do not always define "quality" in the same way their customers do. Too often companies miss critical key customer requirements and instead focus on technical requirements that may be sufficient when viewing products and services in isolation, but which do not please their customers. If your customers are not thrilled with your goods and services, then *all of your products are defective*, no matter what your internal defect rate metrics may say.

No company should ever leave itself in a position where the definition of "quality" it uses differs from that of its customers. A company has to know with certainty how each of its customers will gauge "quality output" before ever quoting new business, and a company has to make sure that this information is communicated clearly throughout the engineering and production processes. Sometimes a better way to think of quality is with the phrase *customer requirements*. As noted earlier, if the customer wants a cup holder in her car, and a car model does not have one, then that is *a defective car*. Why? Because it does not meet its customer's requirements. Please remember that adding cup holders is a job for design engineers, not assembly line workers.

Not knowing what a customer really wants is a paradox that should not exist. If a company asks its customers how they define "quality," as it relates to the goods and services the customer buys from them, the company will find that most of its customers are more than happy to answer. Customers may also describe what they do not define as "quality," which is just as useful; adding things your customers do not want is a form of waste.

It is also important to understand exactly how goods and services are used, and for how long. It is wasteful to make a product that lasts three years if it will be thrown away in two, and at the same time, if a particular product needs to last two years and it breaks in twenty-three months, that is low quality. The length of time a customer expects a product to last can be called its "usage point." If, for example, people want to upgrade a cell phone every two years, the "usage point" for those cell phones would be two years. We can measure how long a company's products last against that usage point and make a bell curve. The narrower the bell curve (the less variation), the easier it is to have a high level of quality without a high

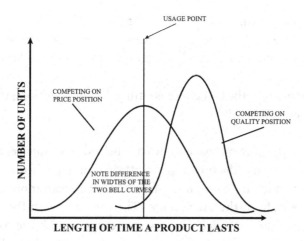

FIGURE 9.1
The Breakage Bell Curve

amount of waste. Some call this "planned obsolescence," but really it is just smart business. When we graph this, we get a "breakage bell curve" (Figure 9.1).

Companies need to understand their role in the market against the roles of their competitors. If a company is the low-cost provider, it does not make sense to also try to be the high-quality provider, unless both metrics really can be met.

The breakage bell curve is related to cost. A company should map-out that relationship so that they can see how much quality they can produce at different price points. If someone knows what they are capable of in terms of quality at different price points, as well as where their competitors are positioned, they can carve out the proper balance based on the competitive position being sought. The high-quality position is the one where the mean of the breakage bell curve is three sigma away from the usage point so that virtually all products produced do not break until after they are no longer in use. The low price point is going to be where the mean of the breakage bell curve is almost on top of the usage point.

The width of the bell curves shows how much variance there is in how long products last. A wide bell curve indicates that some items break relatively quickly, whereas others last a very long time. Imagine a company that makes cell phones where some start to break after a week, and others last ten years. These cell phones would have a very wide bell curve. A narrow bell curve indicates that virtually all items break at around the same time.

How far to the right the bell curve is situated shows how long the average item lasts before it breaks.

The graph on the previous page shows two bell curves – one very wide bell curve with the mean (the breakage point) right on top of the usage point, and another, much narrower bell curve, with the mean more than three sigma to the right of the usage point. The company with the wider bell curve is competing on price whereas the company with the narrow bell curve is competing on quality. As it is difficult to move three sigma from the usage point with a wide breakage bell curve, this company has also invested in making the bell curve narrower.

The ideal position to be in would be to have the narrow bell curve to the right of the usage point, and to be able to hold that position at the lowest cost. If the company competing on price cannot sell for less than the company competing on quality, the company competing on price is going to go out of business.

Neither bell curve is "better" or "worse" than the other. What is "Better" and "Worse" vary by market segment. One bell curve is geared toward a higher quality product, and the other is (hopefully) geared toward a lower price. The "better" position is whichever market segment a company can dominate.

Something else to consider is that either of these companies could potentially erode the other's market share by encroaching upon the other. If the higher quality company reduced its quality some, and then was able to lower its price, it might be able to take sales from the other company, by offering what is still a higher level of quality, but at a price point closer to the competitor.

Conversely, the lower quality company might be able to take market share from the higher quality company, simply by making its bell curve narrower, so that its products start to break closer to the usage point.

Industries change over time. It is important to choose positions relative to those of competitors, and to periodically revisit chosen positions against the changing positions of competitors.

As a general rule, using lean techniques will increase quality while decreasing variability, making breakage bell curves narrower, while simultaneously pushing them to the right. That's obviously a good thing, but don't slide to the right unintentionally, and don't slide to the right so much that what is being made is at a higher level of quality than customers want. Excessive quality is a form of waste.

An example of excessive quality: a leader of R&D at the HP Printer Division once challenged his R&D engineers by standing on one of the printers during a meeting. "Who has a customer that needs a printer strong enough to support 200 pounds?" he asked. Nobody. Extra engineering time and effort and extra material went into making the printer body that strong. It did not improve print quality or speed, which customers *did want*. Therefore a strong body did not add value for the customer. Reducing the body strength sped up the design process for new printers and saved on raw materials during manufacturing.

The goal with quality is the same as the goal in every other aspect of business – to build products that meet customer needs better, and cheaper, than can anyone else, thereby outperforming competitors

10

Supply Chain Management

Companies tend to focus primarily on things that happen within their own four walls, but even small changes in demand can cause confusion as those changes work their way down supply chains, creating bullwhip-like oscillations between suppliers producing too much, and too little. Economists call this effect "Forester's Whip," after the economist who first documented it, and Harvard has a game they play called "The Beer Game" (YouTube it) where the effect is demonstrated. The oscillation grows in size and severity as it moves farther down the supply chain, and there is a direct correlation between the amount of inventory in a supply chain and the severity of the whip-like effect.

When people say that free markets cause boom and bust cycles, really it is Forester's Whip, and in theory if companies could remove all inventory from their supply chains (or achieve perfect visibility of inventory levels and actual demand), they could end the boom and bust cycle.

Note too that Forester's Whip does not cause recessions. In a diverse free-market economy, each industry has its own boom and bust cycle, with different companies, and different industries, at different points in the cycle, at different times. It takes a systemic shock to plunge an entire economy into a bust cycle, and only three forces are capable of creating such a shock: unexpected changes in the value of money, government policies, and natural disasters (including diseases like COVID-19). People love to blame free markets for recessions, citing them as "market failures," but unless an economy lacks diversity, free markets are incapable of causing recessions. Recessions are, in almost all cases, caused by government tampering.

Forester's whip injects costs throughout a supply chain, and these costs invariably find their way to the top. As such, companies with long supply chains and/or lots of inventory in their supply chains often have significant unnecessary costs. Giving visibility of changes in demand, and taking steps to reduce the need for inventory throughout the supply chain, can reduce this effect, and reduce costs significantly. In some industries, Forester's Whip may be the single largest source of cost in a supply chain, so don't take the savings potential lightly.

The most important thing to remember about supply chain management is that any costs, or savings, incurred anywhere in the supply chain, invariably make their way to the top. We all know this to be true on some level, but it is worth bearing out, as many indicate that they have no emotional connection with this fact, by treating costs their suppliers incur, as somehow separate from costs that they incur.

If a company sells something to Walmart, and Walmart then says they want a new discount, the company selling to Walmart may sell at a loss for a time, while struggling to reduce costs. Walmart is, in fact, banking on their suppliers' abilities to reduce costs, whenever they press for a new discount.

BE CAREFUL WHAT YOU INCENTIVIZE

If people think Walmart is bad, they should try Home Depot. I have not worked with Home Depot in years, but in the late 90s and early 2000s, Home Depot's buyers had a bonus program in which, whenever they had a line review (where all manufacturers who make a particular product compete for business), if the buyer could not get a price reduction from the current manufacturer, the buyer got a bigger bonus for going to a new supplier *even if the new supplier had a higher price* than the current supplier. Buyers would actually change suppliers for a higher price before they would stay with an existing supplier at the same price *even if the existing supplier's price was lower*. The reason the buyers' bonus took a hit if they could not get a price reduction from existing suppliers (and no hit if they changed suppliers), was to place pressure on the existing supplier to continually lower pricing, whether doing so was still possible or not. The assumption was that the supplier could always find another corner to cut, and if not there is always another supplier ready to step in – maybe from China.

Many badly designed incentive systems incentivize the wrong behavior or produce unintended consequences. My colleague Mike McCarthy tells of a Lean manager in a manufacturing plant who bragged of holding over 40 Kaizen Events in one year. He asked her, "What results improved? On time delivery? Defect rate? Lead time reduced?" She answered, "I don't know, but corporate loved that we held over 40 Kaizen Events!" Obviously she was held accountable for the number of Kaizen (improvement) Events she held, and not for producing results which mattered to customers. This was wasted effort. For more about the right and wrong way to design incentive systems, see Mike McCarthy's book *Sustain Your Gains*[1] ~ *The People Side of Lean Six-Sigma. www.SustainLeanGains.com.*

Incidentally, if a company is in an industry where there is a Chinese competitor ready to step in, then read the section on maturing markets.

While it is true that Walmart and Home Depot have such strong market positions that they can dictate lower prices from suppliers, it is also true that there are suppliers who have made a strategic decision not to sell to Home Depot and Walmart. K-Mart used to think it could tell suppliers how much to charge, and over time K-Mart had fewer and fewer suppliers to choose from. Back when I worked for a company that was struggling to make money selling to Home Depot and Walmart, K-Mart asked us to sell to them. We set the price. K-Mart had no other suppliers left for the products we produced and had no choice but to take the price we set. K-Mart is, of course, going out of business.

FORCED PRICE REDUCTIONS CAN LEAD TO FORCED QUALITY REDUCTIONS

Even for really big retailers, like Walmart and Home Depot, costs incurred anywhere in the supply chain eventually make their way to the top. It is entirely possible for suppliers to pass-on higher costs by reducing the quality of the products sold, and many suppliers of Walmart and Home Depot sell higher quality items through other retailers. When manufacturers do not sell their higher quality products to Walmart and Home Depot, Walmart and Home Depot are essentially paying for the discounts they demand, through lower quality products, and a lack of access to the best products those manufacturers produce.

Walmart and Home Depot take it on faith that if they squeeze their suppliers, their suppliers will find ways to become more efficient. They are operating on the assumption that any *savings* that occur anywhere in the supply chain will eventually make their way to the top, and they are assuming that they can *drive* those savings by arbitrarily reducing what they pay their suppliers. To the degree that they are right, this can be an effective strategy, but to the degree that they are wrong, it causes problems.

I want to stress that I am not against Home Depot or Walmart. Walmart in particular gets blasted regularly on social media for its relatively low wages, but employees just starting out are offered wages that reflect lower skill sets. In the economic expansion of 2017–2019, demand for workers was up. Fast food restaurants, Walmart, and others offered wages above the minimum wage. The law of supply and demand is still in effect. If Walmart is not going to employ people who are just starting out in their working careers, and who have no marketable skills, who will? Pricing people out of work does not help them, and we should salute companies like Home Depot, Walmart, and McDonalds, who are willing to hire people who might otherwise never have the opportunity to work. The climb up the ladder to success must start somewhere, and if the first rung is out of reach, due to some artificial barrier (like a minimum wage), then some people are doomed to a life of dependency on government welfare.

There are very good ways to help the working poor that do not force them into dependency (dependency is not a cure for poverty), but that is outside the scope of this book. For now, suffice it to say that I started at McDonalds, and I salute them for giving me the opportunity. It was my first practical chance to experiment with process improvement, which has proven to be a very valuable skill.

As for quality – if there were no market for disposable items of lower quality, then Walmart and Home Depot would not be able to stay in business without changing strategies.

It is true that savings incurred anywhere in the supply chain invariably make their way to the top. If a company is as big as Home Depot or Walmart, then they really can impose the need to find savings, but imposing cost reductions did not *make* Walmart and Home Depot dominant players. Rather, Walmart and Home Depot only began to impose lower prices on their suppliers *after* they became dominant players, and while Walmart is still the world's biggest retailer (at least as of the time of this writing), their lead is shrinking. As for Home Depot, they used to be the second-largest retailer in the United States, but today Costco, Kroger, Walgreens, and Amazon are larger than Home Depot. The growth of Target and Lowes are directly related to the policies of Walmart and Home Depot. Essentially, what Walmart and Home Depot are doing is cashing in their size for short-term profit at the expense of long-term growth. What they are growing in the long term are not their profits, but their competitors.

Thirty years earlier, K-Mart did the same thing. There is a pattern at play.

There is another factor in Home Depot's and Walmart's ability to use their size to force suppliers to reduce pricing: even when it works, the benefit tends to be transitory.

As an example, let us say a company makes widgets. This company sells widget A to Walmart, and widget B to a smaller retailer. This company sells millions of dollars' worth of widgets to Walmart a year, and only a few thousand to the smaller retailer, so obviously Walmart has more leverage over this company than does the smaller retailer. The company makes more profit selling to the smaller retailer (at least per sale), but Walmart's volumes are such that losing Walmart as a customer is a non-starter.

Let's say Walmart suddenly says they want a new 1.5% discount. The company was barely eking any profit on Walmart to begin with, so this is a problem at first, but the company is able to find some waste in their processes, and they return to profitability with a 1.5% lower price.

That's great for Walmart, but, unless the waste the company found was only related to the widgets it made for Walmart, they can also charge the smaller retailer 1.5% less.

Having a giant customer like Walmart allows a company to negotiate lower material costs from their suppliers, by letting them order much larger quantities of raw materials than they would need without that demand. Someone might think that this gives Walmart an advantage over other retailers, but the lower raw material costs affect everything the company makes, including the things sold to smaller retailers.

Competitive pressures tend to force suppliers to pass along cost savings to *all* retailers.

WORK WITH (NOT AGAINST) SUPPLIERS TO REDUCE COSTS VIA PROCESS IMPROVEMENTS

The right way for a company (any company) to work with suppliers on ways to reduce costs is to encourage their suppliers to change *their* operations in ways that add value and reduce cost. In other words, companies should *encourage suppliers to do some of the things mentioned in this book.* The savings will make those suppliers dominant players in *their* respective industries, and, as all savings anywhere in the supply chain eventually make it to the top, their savings will eventually become everyone's savings, including the consumers'.

My colleague Mike McCarthy tells of a buyer with one of his clients who knew how to do it right. The buyer offered his suppliers long term contracts. In year one, the price per unit would be 5% *above* the current price. In year two, the price would go back to the base year price. In year three, the unit price would be 4% below the base year price. In year four, the unit price would be 7% below the base year price. In year five, the unit price would be 10% below the base year price. The understanding was that the supplier would use the extra money in year one to finance process improvements that would allow it to deliver cost reductions in years three, four, and five. A win–win for both parties.

Toyota is smart. Toyota works with their suppliers, utilizing lean techniques, to reduce costs. Toyota looks long term, ensuring that suppliers are profitable and that supplier concerns are heard. Toyota builds partnerships with their supplier base, looking at the entire supply chain as a unified team with a unified goal: delivering better cars at better prices to the consumer. Everything in the supply chain is geared toward consumer value, and as such, Toyota and its supplier base are aligned with society at large, making profit a natural byproduct of operations. Toyota even likes to buy partial ownership in their suppliers as a reflection of the long-term nature of the relationship.

Working in partnership with suppliers helps to pull costs out of the supply chain, without also growing the competition. While this route may be more work, and may not be as profitable in the short term, in the long run it enhances rather than inhibits a company's competitive position.

Whatever savings a company gets from its suppliers will of course end up going to anyone else who uses the same suppliers, but because the savings are real rather than imposed, and because *all* of a company's suppliers will have the same kinds of lower costs, all the way down the supply chain (assuming the company pushes these techniques all the way down its supply chain), unless competitors have *all* of the same suppliers, those lower costs *will* provide a competitive advantage.

I have a sneaky suspicion that one of the reasons Toyota likes to buy partial ownership of suppliers is to ensure that Toyota's competitors don't get to use all of the same suppliers Toyota uses.

Compare Walmart's technique to Toyota's. Walmart continuously imposes discounts and price reductions on their supply chain, without doing anything to make those lower prices and discounts possible. They end up with a round-robin of suppliers, all of whom cut whatever corners they can, including on quality, to make a buck in spite of the price reductions and discounts demanded. Toyota, on the other hand, is obsessive about actual improvement, and works with suppliers to help them improve. As improvements are made, Toyota asks for some of the savings, but they allow their suppliers to stay profitable, and because the improvements are cumulative, they are able to reduce costs more and more every year, even as quality keeps getting better rather than worse.

Walmart and Home Depot are, of course, doing what they do because they are focused on their short term profitability. Toyota is focusing on its *competitive position* instead. That is the real difference. Toyota knows is that if a company takes care of its *competitive position*, profits will take care of themselves.

Many Deming followers call running a company by such measurables as profit margin, "driving looking only in the rearview mirror," and this is an apt metaphor. Profitability does not show what a company is doing, so much as what it did do in the past. Assuming that because something was profitable in the past, it will remain profitable in the future, assumes that nothing changes. If that were a safe assumption to make, then driving a car looking only in the rearview mirror would be safe, for if someone were on the road before, and nothing changed, they would stay on the road. Eventually in business, just as in driving, we will encounter a turn and a tree, and if we are not looking forward, we will crash.

One nice thing about business is that the forward thinking company gets to control the competitive landscape. When a company is out in front, they get to decide where the turns and the trees are. Think Apple with the iPhone. Steve Jobs gave consumers something they did not know they wanted until they saw it. And no competitor had anything like it for over 22 months.

Some will argue that profits are important, and must be monitored. I agree, just as I agree that one should occasionally look at the rearview mirror when driving a car. However, the purpose of watching profitability is the same as the purpose of looking in the rearview mirror: to see what is coming up from behind. It is valuable to know what is coming up from behind (competitors), but it is more valuable to know what is coming up ahead: new products that will yield better profits.

Companies should work with their suppliers to improve operations, while also protecting supplier profitability. A supplier willing to improve is worth far more in the long run than is a supplier with a lower price for the next sixth months.

Try to spread this culture down the entire supply chain.

NOTE

1 *Sustain Your Gains*, Michael McCarthy, Performance Management Publications, 2011.

11

Human Resources

"Human Resources" is not a department, though a company may have a department by that name. "Human Resources," rather, are employees. Before we discuss what the department by this name should be doing, we need to discuss what employees are, and how to treat them.

There is a tendency to look at employees as costs and then to try to minimize that cost. To a point this makes sense: Karl Marx argued that one definition of "profit" is the difference between what all of the employees within a company produce, and what they are paid. That definition leaves out the role of the inventor who creates what is then produced from his or her ideas. As an example, iPhones did not exist twenty years ago. Steve Jobs invented the iPhone, creating tens of thousands of jobs.

It is true that the less a company pays its employees, the more profit it will make. This works in the short term, but as employees gain skills, they will take those skills to better-paying employers. The flip-side is far more true: the more a set number of employees produce, the more profit a company will make. The trick then is not to pay the most, nor the least, but to maximize the difference between what employees are paid, and what they make.

THE MARKET SETS PRICES AND WAGES

Companies don't really control what they pay their employees. Each company competes for labor in an open market, just as they compete for every other resource. While companies can choose to pay more or less than average, no company sets the market price. There is also a correlation between what a company pays, compared to the average for a given type of labor, and the quality of the employees that company is able to hire. Taco Bell recently advertised that a manager could make $100,000!

Somehow the notion that companies do not dictate wages is controversial in some political circles. That's always struck me as odd. The current market price for a two-foot piece of steel rebar is between $1.40 and $1.84, depending on thickness. If companies could set whatever price they want for labor, they could also set whatever price they want for steel. Steel producers would love to make more than $1.40–$1.84 for steel rebar, and steel consumers would love to pay less. Neither of them decides. The market sets the price. There is a McDonalds near where I live advertising jobs at $11 an hour, so the current market-clearing price for labor must be somewhere near that level. McDonalds does not set that price (nor does Walmart). If companies set the price for labor, they'd pay less. The government *can* set the price, but only by imposing a minimum that prices some labor out of the workforce.

Employees do not control what they can charge a company for their services either. Employees compete for work in the same market in which companies compete for labor, and in any negotiation, both sides are going to take a price somewhere within the relatively narrow band set by the market.

ONE BAD CEO CAN PUT A COMPANY OUT OF BUSINESS

Some think that if CEOs made less, then entry-level workers would make more, but that too is untrue. CEOs are not competing for the same positions entry-level workers are and are thus not in the same labor market. Having one bad entry-level worker makes very little difference to overall company performance, whereas having the wrong CEO could cause a company to go out of business. CEOs get paid what they get paid because of the importance of having the right skills in that role, and their pay has absolutely nothing to do with what anyone else makes. If anything, having the right CEO can help to make a company more profitable, meaning that it can afford to pay entry-level workers more as well.

As companies cannot control the market for labor, their control over the cost of labor is extremely limited. Companies have far more control over how much of their employees' full potential they are able to utilize. Because of this, to maximize profit in the long term, companies need to be able to attract and retain motivated, talented employees. They need to motivate those employees to contribute as much as they can.

Companies that expect employees to be thankful for their employment have a much harder time retaining talent than do companies who are thankful to have talent worth retaining.

Employees generally view themselves as people who trade labor for pay, and as such, most employees, rather than being thankful for being employed, simply look at their pay as compensation for their services. Companies that expect employees to be thankful for their employment have a much harder time retaining talent than do companies who are thankful to have talent worth retaining.

Managers who try to *push* employees to work harder usually fail. *Leaders*, however, *ask* team members to join a process improvement team and help with their ideas. This shows respect for the employee. *When asked* to help, employees generally respond with ideas and extra effort. Everyone wants to be part of a winning team. This is *pull* leadership.[1] With the right leader, employees learn to motivate themselves. The role of management is to remove obstacles that prevent employees from self-motivating.

Managers can build motivating environments, and particularly when managers put the organization, and its employees, ahead of themselves. Doing so generates trust and loyalty. Many employees say, "I loved the company, but I quit because of my boss."

THE ROLE OF PAY AND BENEFITS

Pay and benefits are a primary factor in determining which employees leave and which employees stay (other primary factors include management and geography). When employees are comparing positions, they tend to monetize benefits and to choose the employer who offers the most competitive *combined* pay and benefits *package.* In this way, employees view benefits as a part of their pay rather than something above and beyond pay. When benefits are improved, employees look at it as a raise, and when benefits are reduced, employees look at it as a pay-cut. When employees face what they perceive as a pay-cut, their natural belief is that they are still worth what they were paid prior to the cut. Because employees view benefit reductions as a form of pay-cut, when a company reduces benefit packages without a corresponding increase in pay, it encourages employees to leave.

Companies with higher pay, and lower benefits, tend to attract younger, single employees, who are more apt to value pay than benefits. Companies with lower pay, and better benefits, tend to attract older employees with families – people for whom security is as important as pay. Companies with both higher pay, and better benefits, attract everyone. Companies with both lower pay, and lower benefits, attract those employees who lack either the skills, or the attitudes, to be able to find jobs with better employers.

Companies that pay less than competitive wages and benefits attract two types of employees: those who lack the skills necessary to do their jobs, and those with personality defects which make them unemployable at competitive rates. When a low-paying company gets lucky, and attracts a good employee (usually someone young and inexperienced for the position offered), the tendency is to over-burden that employee with all of the work less competent employees cannot do, or that problematic employees will not do. The result is that companies who pay below market rates can't *keep* good employees, even when they are lucky enough to *find* them.

EMPOWERMENT FOR RETENTION

Empowerment is another factor in employee retention. When employees feel as if their talents are not valued, they become demotivated. When employees feel that their decisions and talents contribute to company success, they take a much more active stake in company operations, and perform at a higher level. Who makes employees feel this way? Their boss. This is Pull Leadership.

Companies need to encourage employees to be problem-solvers, coaching them, such that they learn from mistakes, by fostering an environment where employees feel they can come up with innovative and creative solutions, to whatever problems might be encountered. This is a primary role of the leader/manager. Companies also have to pay competitive rates, with a competitive benefit package. If a company wishes to increase the average level of talent, that company has to increase pay and/or benefit levels. Wages for all employees should be looked at periodically. If a business wants to keep an employee, it should keep that employee at competitive pay and benefit levels at all times. If a business wants to encourage an employee to leave, it should let their pay and benefits lag behind the market, or fire them for cause.

Personally, I believe in paying the market average salary for employees, and then using a profit-sharing bonus targeted at 20% of salary on top of that. A company won't pay each employee the average amount, since some employees will have higher than average skills and experience, and others will have lower levels of skill and experience, but a company should aim to be around the average when looking at the company as a whole. The 20% profit-sharing bonus pushes the employer into the "better paying" category, but only in years where the company makes a profit.

Profit sharing will retain talented employees in the long run, but it will not motivate them day to day. For tips on leadership skills, read Chapter 5 of *Sustain your Gains*, by Michael McCarthy.

It should go without saying that all employees should be treated with dignity and respect at all times, but somehow that does not go without saying. If a manager really does have an employee that does not deserve dignity and respect, that employee should be fired. Even when an employee is fired, they should be shown dignity and respect through the firing process. If a company has a manager that has trouble treating employees with dignity and respect, the company should put them in a non-managerial role, find them additional managerial training, or fire them for cause.

HUMAN RESOURCES, THE DEPARTMENT

Now that we have discussed what human resources are, and how they should be treated, let us discuss what a company's Human Resources Department should be doing.

A company's Human Resources department needs to work with employees, rather than against them, as an advocate of both the company and the employee. HR's job is also (as experts on labor law) to prevent the company from making mistakes that could make the company liable in court.

HR has a role in preserving and protecting the culture of the organization. As the culture of an organization should be chosen and planned, HR has to look for anything that might change the culture in an unintended way. With regard to company policies, the question should not only be, "is this policy legal and/or does it create any legal liability," but also, "what will the impact on the culture of the organization be if this policy is implemented, and what changes might be made to foster the desired culture?"

Motivation is a part of a company's culture, and all cultural changes occur as a ground swell from the bottom up. While management can, and should, determine the culture an organization is going to take, no manager can *force* a culture to be adopted by executive decree. Managers can *do* things, and can implement policies, that *encourage* a ground swell that will move culture in the intended direction, and Human Resources can monitor that ground swell and help managers throughout the organization, from top to bottom, behave in ways that foster the desired culture, but managers cannot simply mandate that a given culture emerge. As noted above, mandating is "push" leadership. If creating the correct culture were as easy as mandating that it happen, changing cultures would be easy. Instead, the vast majority of companies that try to change cultures fail to do so.

Taiichi Ohno did not get the culture he wanted at Toyota by spelling the new culture out in a memo. He did so by making changes on the plant floor that impacted people's every day jobs in ways that reflected the culture he wanted. The ground swell naturally followed, but it was not easy, and Taichi Ohno is the exception rather than the norm. Most managers do not make the kind of commitment to cultural change that Taichi Ohno did, and because of this most cultural changes become the kind of managerial failures I discuss in Strategic Decision Making.

Managers can change the culture of their organizations (or the parts of organizations they manage), but it takes more than an executive order. It takes "pull" leadership whereby you *ask* employees to sign on to this new culture of process improvement. Managers must become a part of the new culture, and must lead the new culture changes until the changes ripple out to the rest of the company.

Ironically, a bad manager can create a bad culture almost overnight. It is always easier to break a complicated system than to improve upon them. The same is true with a company's culture.

All it takes is one bad manager and a part of a company will not be customer-centric. This will impact other departments in negative ways, and ripple through the entire organization. Most Human Resources departments spend most of their time working with employees who do not follow company policy, but with the right culture in place, that should be a rare occurrence. Human resources should instead work with higher level managers to help improve the managerial skills of lower-level managers to prevent problems from arising.

HR should define the policies for mentoring, and for manager succession. HR should monitor the company, such that when company policies are not being implemented, the proper people know about it. HR should also act in a supporting role, helping managers train and coach other managers, when necessary – HR should never become some kind of managerial gestapo.

The actual training of new managers, and the grooming of lower level managers into higher level managers, is not an HR function, but is a function of the managers throughout the organization (there is also a role for HR in training when the training is not specific to an individual job). HR has no role as "manager police" either, so there is no place for HR to punish managers who are not managing correctly. HR should, however, monitor such things, and should, if necessary, make sure higher-level managers know when there is a problem.

Another major role of human resources is to ensure that there is a steady progression of leadership throughout the organization. Managers need to be teaching others to be managers, so that as managers get promoted (or leave the organization), there are people readily available to step up and take their place. A manager's first job is the same as anyone else's: to eliminate the need for their current role. With the right culture, where employees believe that eliminating the need for what they are currently doing will lead to a promotion rather than discharge, companies will get employees who want to make the company as lean as possible.

HR should also be the primary group looking at employee wages, to keep them competitive.

If a company does these things, both in terms of how employees are hired and treated, as well as in terms of what HR does, the culture of the organization, and the attitudes of the employees, will become the company's greatest strategic asset.

NOTE

1 For more on Pull Leadership for process improvement, see *How to Engage, Involve, and Motivate Employees – Building a Culture of Lean Leadership and Two-Way Communication*, by Janis Allen and Michael McCarthy. 2017, Productivity Press.

12

Project Management and On-Time Delivery

Everything in this book will help to reduce lead times. This chapter is about properly quoting delivery dates and managing the plant floor based on the delivery dates quoted.

Companies should not quote delivery times they cannot meet, and yet it is amazing how often they do. When a company starts a job with insufficient time to complete it, people rush, and when people rush, they make mistakes. The earlier a mistake is made (say in sales instead of engineering, or in engineering instead of production), the more costly the mistake is likely to be, making it absolutely critical that companies understand, not only customer requirements but also their own internal lead times. It is absolutely critical that sales departments utilize this information to quote delivery times companies are capable of meeting. The old adage of "under promise and over deliver" endures.

When it is necessary to quote times that a company cannot meet, that company should involve project management, using the Program Evaluation and Review Technique (PERT), to gauge both the potential for compressing critical timelines as well as the costs involved.

PERT, in a nutshell, is a technique that looks not only at what tasks need to be done, but also at when they need to be done. Most tasks have a variance between the earliest point when it is possible to start them, and the point where if they are not started, it will cause late shipments. Tasks that have the same date, as both the earliest and latest start dates, are called "critical timeline events." When using PERT, a company prioritizes doing things that are on the critical timeline above doing things that are not (Figure 12.1).

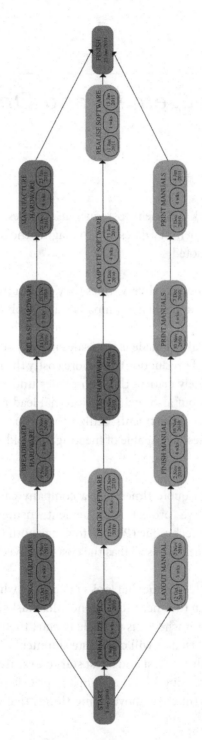

FIGURE 12.1
PERT Chart

In the PERT Chart example above, the items in darker grey represent the critical timeline, as all of these items need to start on the first day it is possible to start them, or the completion date will be pushed out. The items in lighter grey all take less time than is available to do them, and starting them as soon as possible is not as important as it is for the critical timeline events.

One can make a PERT Chart manually, and it's a good practice to do so at least once, just to understand exactly how PERT methodology works. Start with the last item, which will be something like, "Finish" or "Ship," and work backward, listing all of the tasks that have to be done before the last task can be done. Keep listing tasks, working backward, until the start of the project is reached. While listing tasks, draw lines to specify which tasks have to be done before other tasks can be started. Specify on each task how long it will take to complete, as well as the date the task has to start by, based on the length of time the task will take to complete, to make the project completion date. As an example, if a project has to be completed by February 1, and the last task before completion will take three days, then that task will have to start no later than January 29 for a February 1 completion to be possible.

WHICH TASK DO THE OTHERS DEPEND ON?

Once all of the tasks have been listed working backward, start at the first task and move forward, writing down the first date it is possible to start each task, based on the dependencies between tasks. As an example, if task B cannot be started until task A is complete, and task A starts on January 1 and takes four days, then the earliest task B can be started, is January 5.

Once all tasks have both the first date it is possible to start them, as well as the last date they must be started by, note that many tasks can be started earlier than they have to be. The gap between when a task *can* be started, and when it *has to* be started, is called "slack time." Where the earliest and latest start dates are the same, those events have no slack time and are on the critical timeline. Critical timeline tasks have to be started as quickly as possible, or the project will not finish on time.

Project management programs, like Microsoft Project, or Project Libre (which is free), can do much of the work of making PERT Charts. I highly recommend using a project program, as projects can become far more complex than the example above, and project management software automates much of the work.

INTELLIGENT RESOURCE ALLOCATION

A company will likely have many projects all occurring at the same time. If that company knows the critical timelines, they can allocate resources accordingly, focusing on critical timeline events across all projects, and doing non-critical timeline events at a lower priority.

It is often possible to compress critical timelines by throwing more resources at the right places, and if a customer has the need for a compressed lead time, they might be willing to pay to compress it. It is also likely that if a company can show its customers a methodology used to quote lead times, those customers will have more faith in the company's ability to meet its commitments.

Sometimes more resources cannot compress the time needed to produce. The old adage taught in Project Management courses is "You can't hire 9 women to make a baby in 1 month."

It costs money to get customers, and the amount of money it costs is often directly related to the expense of the products a company makes. After a company has spent money to get a customer, it makes little sense to lose them because of missed commitments. When a company loses a customer because they missed what, for the customer, was a crucial delivery date, that customer is likely gone forever.

When companies make delivery commitments they cannot meet, they are lying, and there is no other way to put it. If sales people are telling customers whatever they want to hear, with no regard for reality, then those sales people are lying to their customers, and over time, customers are smart enough to figure that out. Microsoft got a bad reputation for missing release dates, and its software upgrades were often called "vaporware."

Think about it from the customer's perspective. Let's say the customer needs something delivered by June 1st. Let us also assume there are two companies the customer is considering, and these two companies made equal price bids. Let's say, furthermore, that not getting the product by June 1st will cost the customer one million dollars a day after that date. The customer asks both companies when they can deliver. Company "A" says, "When would you like us to deliver?" and when the customer tells them they need it by June 1st they say, "No problem. We can ship it on May 31st and have it there the next day." Company "B" says, "We can ship it by June 15th," and when the customer says they need it fifteen days earlier, this company says, "Well, we might be able to compress our time-line, but we might not be able to meet our cost quote if we do." Company "B" then pulls out charts showing exactly how long each part of the process will take, what the critical timeline is, and what parts of the critical timeline they can compress, along with the additional cost of each compression.

After some work, Company "B" is able to commit to a June 1st delivery, but in the process their bid is now $750,000 more than Company "A," reflecting the additional costs they will incur to meet the required delivery date.

Finally, let's assume that Company "B" has an outstanding reputation for meeting commitments – the best in the business for coming through as promised – whereas Company "A" has a reputation, not only for being late, but for sometimes being *really* late.

Which company sounds like the better one to buy from?

Everyone should answer Company "B." The customer is guaranteed to pay a $750,000 premium if it goes with Company "B," but with a late penalty of $1 *million* a day, that $750,000 premium is nothing compared to the cost of missing the delivery date by more than a day.

The Induction heating company I worked for made machines that were all built with unique requirements, making each build essentially a prototype. Our sales team promised whatever the customer wanted to hear, both on price and on delivery dates, and the company generally got the jobs nobody else wanted, at prices nobody else was willing to take. The General Manager and I decided to measure on-time shipping performance over the previous year, and we found that on average the company shipped six months late. That's on average. Some shipments were a *year* late. And don't get me started on rework in the field after the shipment occurred!

After one year, we had the average days late down to three weeks, and nothing was going out more than three months late. Most of the improvement was driven by using the PERT methodology.

I began sitting in toward the end of the quoting process with a copy of Microsoft Project and began developing PERT charts that would show what we were actually capable of achieving, taking into account other projects on the floor. Sales then knew what we *could* do before they made promises. They still made promises we could not keep, but by a smaller margin.

Another improvement we made, which had a huge impact, was to use Critical Timeline PERT methodology to control the plant floor, prioritizing critical timeline events above other items, for all projects on the floor. I had a production meeting every day in which we updated the previous day's PERT charts, and then re-calculated the critical timelines so that the plant knew exactly what had to be accomplished. The number of days it took, on average, to ship product (from the sales close date to the ship date) was cut in *half*.

Note that the critical timeline can shift. If, for example, a process has ten days of slack time, and it is not started for eleven days, it'll become a critical timeline event, and other events that were on the critical timeline before may fall off the critical timeline. A company, then, can't just do a PERT chart at the start of a project and call it done. A company has to constantly update the PERT chart based on what actually occurs on the plant floor, and has to look for changes in the critical timeline.

In repetitive manufacturing, PERT charts are still helpful, but are more helpful for product launches, process changes, product changes, and other kinds of projects that may impact the plant floor, but are not a part of repetitive manufacturing operations. In repetitive manufacturing, a company needs to know its total throughput, its lead times, and its upcoming demand. A company calculates ship dates differently in repetitive manufacturing, but the need to do those calculations, and to be honest about them with customers, is the same. In repetitive manufacturing, a company might be able to outsource parts of its operation or add people to particular areas, to shorten lead times (particularly where there are bottlenecks). A company also might be able to use overtime if its plants do not run 24×7.

13

Strategic Decision Making

Executive teams should meet periodically to discuss short-term, medium-term, and long-term business strategies, and should publish those strategies to all business units and subsidiaries. Subsidiaries and business units should then come up with strategies that support the corporate strategies. Strategies should filter down, from the top of the organization to the bottom, with each level of the company crafting policies that support higher level strategies, and then submitting lower level strategies back up through the chain of command. Strategies filter down from the top, and specific action items in support of strategies filter back up for approval. Ideally, each employee will be tasked with specific action items they can accomplish, in support of overall company goals. Employees can then be held accountable for achieving those goals. This is called "alignment" of strategies from top to bottom.

Most corporate strategies are never truly implemented. Usually, the CEO of an organization either comes up with a strategy or helps develop one with his or her executive team. This strategy is discussed at length among the executive team, but the executives then go back to their offices and do whatever it was they were doing before. Some of them may be in favor of the strategy, and some may even start to implement it within their groups, whereas other executives will not like the strategy, and, while supporting it verbally, will actively work to undermine it. Some executives will sit back and watch to see whether or not the strategy is going to take hold before doing anything, and will only support the strategy if it appears to be gaining ground. Support on the executive team is usually mixed, and at any rate, strategies rarely go much further than the executive team.

There is only one place where a strategy can take effect, and that is where the rubber meets the road. Any strategy that does not impact the value stream of a company, and that does not manifest itself, in some way, in the company Gemba, is not really a strategy at all. A new marketing strategy that does not involve improving products is not a strategy. It's just a sales ploy. A new push on sales is not a strategy. The sales team was (hopefully) pushing before.

New products are strategies. Entering a new industry is a strategy, and particularly if a company is willing to make product changes to support the new industry (which will invariably use the company's products differently than the old industry did).

For example, the camera company Canon produced digital cameras before Kodak did (Kodak actually invented the digital camera, but was stuck in its mature market for film. They missed the chance to develop a new market segment. Review Chapter Five on Maturing Markets.). Now that everyone has a camera in their phones, Canon has moved to medical imaging.

Eliminating waste can be a strategy if the company is serious enough about it, and if it uses bottom-up techniques, like Kaizen events and value-stream mapping, to find waste. Changing a company's culture is a strategy, *if* the company does in fact change its culture rather than just talking about doing so.

WHAT WILL WE DO DIFFERENTLY TO SUPPORT THIS STRATEGY?

One question that has to be asked when making a strategy is "what are we going to do differently to support this strategy?" That's a question that has to be asked at every level of the company, and particularly at the bottom, where production occurs.

Another very important question to ask when making a strategy, is, "why." Keep asking "why" until the root reason this strategy was chosen is found. This will help fine tune that strategy. Here is a hypothetical exchange:

Sales Executive "I think our strategy should be a new sales program to boost sales."

CEO "Why?"

Sales Executive "Because our sales are too low to support operations. We need to fix that."

CEO "Why are our sales too low?"

Sales Executive "Because our quality is too low and our prices are higher than the market will bear."

CEO "Why is our quality too low, and why are our prices too high?"

In this brief exchange, the question "why" has only been asked three times, but already we can see that a new sales program is not going to fix the underlying issues of quality and pricing (Figure 13.1). The lack of sales was

FIGURE 13.1
Root Cause Analysis

not a root cause, but a symptom of quality and pricing issues. Continuing to ask why might lead to ideas on how to improve the quality and price of the items this company makes.

In many companies, the sales team would not know if the quality is too low, or the price too high. Many companies do not ask customers why they did not get selected over other companies. Many companies make assumptions about such things or make excuses. Assumptions and excuses do not lead to solutions, but to mistakes.

Toyota suggests that a company ask "why" five times – they call this "Five Why Analysis." The number "five" is arbitrary, but Toyota believes that if you ask "why" five times, you should at least be close to root causes.

I sometimes catch myself using the term "Five Why Analysis," but I prefer the term "Root Cause Analysis," as "Root Cause Analysis" clarifies that the goal is to ask "why" until the root causes are found. How many times one has to ask "why" to get to the root causes is irrelevant. The point is to deal with root causes rather than symptoms.

DON'T WORK ON SYMPTOMS – FIND ROOT CAUSES

Good strategies start with the solutions to a company's problems, and you cannot solve problems unless you know what they are. Don't work on symptoms – fix the underlying issues the symptoms signify.

As someone asks "why," the answers will often not be in the board room. Executives may *think* they know the root causes (and sometimes they may be right), but executives are somewhat removed from the activities where the rubber meets the road, and it is common for executives to make assumptions. Sales and marketing should be working closely with customers and potential customers to know *exactly* why customers do not always pick their products. Price and quality issues are best found on the plant floor, by asking the people who actually build the product where the quality problems are, and where the waste is. In other words, to get the answers, one has to go to the Gemba. If the root issue is that a company's products do not do what the customers need them to do, then the problem is with engineering.

SHOULD THE CEO MOW THE GRASS?

Speaking of the Gemba, when was the last time executives spent a day working in it? Everyone in an organization should spend a few weeks working on the plant floor when they start with a company, and should periodically spend a day on the floor working directly in the company value stream. If someone runs a landscaping company, go out and mow grass every once in a while. Doing so won't just help employees become motivated; it will also give executives a much better feel for what exactly it is the company does. One can learn more about quality and price issues spending a day on the floor than a year in the board room. If a company's executives do not spend time on the floor already, sending them there is a strategy to employ right away.

TO GAIN GEMBA EXPERTISE, WORK IN THE GEMBA

I was lucky. Long before I studied Lean Manufacturing, I was a young IT Manager working for a manufacturing company, and our plant floor worked four ten-hour days. During our busy season, it was common for all of us office workers to run a production line on Fridays. I know firsthand how much I learned about what that company did, not by watching the plant floor, or by looking at products we built, but by rolling my sleeves up and helping to build those products myself. There is no substitute in the world for going out and doing whatever it is a company does, whether that is writing computer code, or mowing golf courses. Anyone who thinks they are "above" doing the actual work their company is paid by its customers to do is probably not worth employing.

Strategies start with root-causes, and cause changes on the plant floor, but they must also be strategic, which gets back to the "Maturing Markets" chapter. A company has to understand its market and its strategic place within that market, so that the company is defining "problems" based on the company's strategic position. It could be that the strategic position *is* the problem, or it could be that a company's products are not positioned where the company's strategies say they should be. If a strategic position is based on price, then we should be willing to sacrifice some quality to reduce our price. While we would all love to have both the lowest cost product and the highest quality product (which may be possible using Lean techniques), it may not be possible at this moment. If our strategic position is to have the highest quality product, we should be willing to sacrifice price, at least to a degree, to improve quality. If we wish to have both the highest quality and the lowest price, we might have to consider having two products and two brand names – one for each market segment we wish to hit.

Choosing market segments is important. So is hitting them. As a Marine, my adage is, "One shot, one kill," which I equate to picking the market segments wanted, and then hitting that segment with a bullseye. We talked about breakage point bell curves and usage points under the quality chapter. It is important that a company's breakage point bell curve be centered where the company *wants* it to be, and that the bell curve be as narrow as the company wants to make it. Moving that bell curve and/or making it narrower is a strategic decision, and companies should constantly be reviewing these bell curves in relation to where their competitors are on the same chart.

Understanding the chapter on how markets mature is also critical to strategic thinking. Whether or not a company needs to move to a different quadrant on the quadrant chart, focus more on product innovation or on process innovation, or develop entirely new products – these are all strategic decisions that need to be looked at regularly.

WHAT TO CHANGE IS THE STRATEGY

Some of the things that get called "strategic decision making" on executive teams blow my mind, and if anyone has ever sat in an executive meeting and heard someone say something like, "Ladies and Gentlemen – we are on a burning platform and we have to live to get there," they know what I mean. A burning platform is a change management metaphor. It means companies often won't change until they are in danger of "burning," or going into bankruptcy. Really, when someone starts calling out to burning platforms, what they are presenting is a reason to change, but often without a clear idea of what that change should look like. *What* is such a company going to change? The "what" is the strategy.

"WHERE ARE THE FIREMEN?" "WE LAID THEM OFF!"

Sometimes companies really are on burning platforms. I don't discount that this is sometimes true. In such cases, getting off the burning platform (or rather putting out the fire) should be a tactic and not a strategy. Strategies are not always short, medium, and long term. Sometimes companies have to have an *immediate* term too. But once people realize their company is on a burning platform, they can't just run around yelling "FIRE! FIRE! FIRE!" (as in layoffs – which won't put out the fire but might put the company in a position where it has no firemen). When on a burning platform, start by asking "why" a lot until the root causes are found, and then start to fix the underlying issues. While at it, start to develop a short, medium, and long-term strategy.

If a company does not choose a strategy, the company's competitors will force it into the position where it has to take the jobs nobody else wants, at prices nobody else is willing to accept. The next step usually is bankruptcy.

14

Executive Team Operations

Many organizations make decisions informally, and waste resources on political in-fighting, usually with personal fiefdoms rather than the company's interests at heart. When each executive is pulling the company in a different direction, jockeying favor to gain advantage against other executives, it is impossible to bring different systems into alignment. Organizations can only run efficiently when decisions are made collaboratively, utilizing the collective skills and experience of the entire executive team, in support of the company as a whole.

Disagreement should be encouraged in executive meetings, but once a decision has been made, all members of the executive team must publicly support that decision, no matter what their personal thoughts and beliefs may be. Political in-fighting amongst executives should not be tolerated, and anyone incapable of putting company interests ahead of personal desires should be fired.

There are two common problems that prevent many executives from being effective:

1) They do not believe they have enough time to do their jobs (such as making systemic improvements to processes), so they spend their time doing other things (reacting to problems caused by unimproved processes), and
2) They focus on building up the power of their personal fiefdoms, by playing political games, rather than implementing the goals of the company, by performing value-adding activities.

FIGHT THE COMPETITION, NOT EACH OTHER

Business waged properly involves aggressively seeking market share, and the only reason most businesses have not yet lost is because their competitors are just as weak as they are, with the same executive problems. CEOs have executive meetings with the executive team, and strategic decisions are made. Everyone agrees. And then all of the executives, except the CEO, go back to their offices and work on undermining one another, instead of implementing whatever was supposedly agreed upon. Think of how much more effective companies would be if the executive teams fought their competitors instead of fighting each other.

Another problem common on executive teams is that they often gauge ideas based on who came up with the idea, rather than based on the merit of the idea. This is a side effect of playing politics, as it is political to favor the ideas of those with whom one is currying favor (as well as ideas that will benefit them and their fiefdoms personally), while simultaneously shooting down other ideas that may hinder one's personal fiefdom. They think, "How does this benefit me?" instead of "How does this benefit customers?"

Fiefdom-building executives are particularly dangerous, as they are in a position to undermine the cultural changes companies may be undertaking. Executives who feel threatened by cultural changes may even actively work to undermine those changes. Executives are not likely to call the CEO out directly, but are apt to use passive-aggressive techniques.

Dealing with political in-fighting is easy: fire those who do it. Unfortunately, only the CEO can fire these people (firing sends a message to everyone else: start helping or get out). Everyone else needs tactics for dealing with political infighting (Figure 14.1).

It is an unfortunate fact that the very worst way to get people on board for a decision is to appeal to them based on the decision's merits. The two techniques that work best are personal appeals and deal-making. Each technique works on a different type of person, and as one gets to know people, one will start to pick out what might work with whom.

FIGURE 14.1
Fight the Competition, Not Each Other

Personal appeals are exactly what they sound like: asking someone for help. Essentially, one says, "I have this great idea, but I can't do it without you." This is an appeal for this person to join the project team. This is Pull leadership.

The second technique is to make a deal. A manager might trade support for one initiative for support for another or may structure an idea such that it involves another manager's department in a way that this manager likes. The idea is to bring this kind of person on board by making it in their best interest to do so,

I was a bit miffed when I learned that, statistically, the least effective arguments for getting an idea implemented were those based on the merits of the idea. However, study after study have shown that most managers in most companies simply do not care about the merits of an idea, and while a company CEO should be focused on changing that metric – on building a culture where the merits of an idea are the only thing that count – the reality is that many of the people reading this book will not be CEOs, and will have to deal with managers who do not care about the merits of ideas. This may sound cynical, but study after study have shown it to be true.

GIVE AND TAKE

Sometimes getting support requires a combination of these techniques. When making a personal appeal, someone might ask for something in return. It is even possible that someone who otherwise would have been an adversary will suddenly take an interest in the merits of an idea and look at it with an open mind. The bottom line is that anyone who wants to be effective needs to learn to use a little give and take, making personal appeals, and making deals, when necessary to move good projects forward.

Even in companies where political in-fighting runs rampant, there may be managers who do gauge projects based solely on merit. Latch onto these people as long-term allies, as they are exactly the kinds of managers that help to make businesses stronger.

When making deals, it helps to know how to negotiate. Negotiation is outside the scope of this book, but there is a very good book called *Getting to Yes*,[1] by William Ury, that covers negotiation brilliantly. I strongly recommend that book. A key concept is finding common interests, similar to asking 5 whys.

If you are in a position to change the company culture (and the executive leadership), then put in place an executive team that cares about merit. Choose people who want to work together to achieve the company's strategies. The payback will be immediate.

NOTE

1 *Getting to Yes*, Roger Fisher and William Ury, Penguin Books, 1981.

15

Marketing Operations

In the past, marketing was looked at as an extension of sales. Really, marketing should be considered *a feedback loop* between a company's customers and its engineers, that finds out from customers what the customers want, and then works with the engineers to deliver what the customers have asked for. Marketing ensures that a company's products delight the customer. Marketing then communicates back to the customers, to show them how well the company meets their needs. Marketing provides the eyes and ears from which disruptive products emerge to create new market segments. Think cell phones. Business people needed to call in to the office while traveling. Pay phones were sometimes hard to find. Some marketing person had ears to listen, and voila! Cell phones were born. A whole new market segment.

Using marketing as a feedback loop helps to avoid expensive mistakes. Too many companies think they have a Steve Jobs on staff, with the genius to continuously combine existing technologies in new and innovative ways, to create products that the public will spontaneously buy. For Steve Jobs, this led to iPhones and other remarkable devices, but it can also lead to such disasters as fly-ash shutters and brass fire ant probes. Had the companies checked with their customers, they would have found that there is no demand for shutters that look like concrete, and that the way to kill fire ants is to spray the top of the mound with poison – not to stick a big brass spike into the mound and spray poison on the inside.

I've had ideas I thought were good, such as decorative shutters on quick-release systems, that can be changed whenever a homeowner wants to use a different decoration, or a different color. Imagine being able to, within a few minutes, put up shutters for a favorite team (The University of Michigan in my household), or being able to put up Christmas shutters for the holiday season. Is there demand for such a system? I have no idea, but I would not risk millions of dollars building such a shutter system without first finding out. Sometimes this requires a small market test to see if customers like an idea.

IT BEGINS AND ENDS WITH THE CUSTOMER ALWAYS

One particularly brilliant inventor is Sir James Dyson. He had a number of inventions that achieved very little success until one day he became frustrated with his Hoover vacuum cleaner, which apparently lost power as the bag filled. This led Dyson to begin designing new, innovative vacuum cleaners, but the real key to the story is that the idea came, not from looking at the design of vacuum cleaners in a lab, but by using a vacuum cleaner to clean his own floors. His true innovations were born by using products *as a consumer.* Lean philosophy begins and ends with the customer. Though a given company's customer might be another company, never forget that the customer at the end of the supply chain is a *consumer.*

Just as the people within a company, who perform specific processes all day long, are the people most able to improve those processes, so too those who use goods and services every day are the best ones to determine what they like, and do not like, about those goods and services. Consumers are the best people to determine what kinds of changes might make products better. A company's engineers may be the best equipped to take consumer feedback, and incorporate it into product offerings, but first those engineers need to *have* feedback from the people who use their products in their everyday lives.

Boeing should have involved pilots when designing the safety software for the 737 Supermax, as pilots were the customers of the software.

Engineers do not have the skillsets necessary to gather this information. Engineers do not conduct surveys or focus groups. Marketing people, on the other hand, are the eyes and ears of engineering, interacting with consumers to see how they use products, what they like about them, what they don't like, what they would change or add if they could, what other products they use to accomplish the same things (and what they like and don't like about those products), etc.

Toy companies will often bring in groups of children to play with toys, to see which toys they like, what they like about them, how they play with different toys, and which toys they gravitate to. This is exactly the kind of information producers of any good or service need to have.

With adult goods and services, the same things apply. Companies need to know their customers' needs and desires within the market, as well as what products (including competitor products) they gravitate to, and why. Some companies release "beta versions" of a product under development to "beta testers" who then give feedback about the pros and cons of the new product.

THE SCOUTING PARTY: MARKETING

Rather than being a sub-set of sales, as marketing is often treated, the marketing department should be the "scouting party" of the organization. Nobody in an organization has better data to understand how goods and services are actually used, and how those who use them, *think about them* (compared to other goods and services). Too many companies still think marketing's job is to produce demand rather than to predict it. There is some truth that marketing needs to make marketing materials that stimulate demand, but demand is infinitely easier to stimulate when a company is selling things people actually want. Marketing, more than any other part of an organization, is situated to find out what it is that people want.

A company's sales force needs to work very closely with its marketing team to ensure that the company's sales tactics match its marketing strategy. When sales is detached from marketing, there is a disconnect, making each sale a unique animal that eventually converges on price. Only through a directed marketing message, based on innovative solutions that delight consumers, can a company position itself in the industry as something other than a low-cost provider.

Companies should make products such that customers think, "Yes – that's *exactly* what I was looking for!" Such a reaction is called "customer delight," and it is a competitive advantage.

Clearly, the customer/engineering feedback loop puts marketing in a role where engineering almost reports to it. The relationship between marketing and *sales,* on the other hand, is symbiotic: sales needs to have a message that matches the company's marketing strategy, but if the marketing strategy does not lead to sales, then the marketing strategy is flawed, and more marketing research is needed. In this sense marketing is in a supplier role to sales.

MAKE MARKETING MATERIALS ENTERTAINING

Far too often marketing materials are informative but not fun to read. Nobody is informed by brochures if nobody reads them. If a company has a booth at an event, but that booth is boring, nobody is going to stop by.

The first rule of marketing is not to inform, but to entertain. If materials are entertaining, people will read them. Giving out relevant information is important too, but it has to be done in an entertaining way if any message is going to be given out at all.

DOES ANYBODY RECOGNIZE YOUR BRAND?

Brand recognition is also an important focus of marketing.

When I was working for an induction heating company, I had an idea to make a YouTube channel called, "Induct This." We would have video-taped putting different things into induction heating coils, much like the popular, "Does it Blend" channel. One week, perhaps, we would induction heat an I-Phone. Maybe the next week we would induction heat shotgun shells. Maybe one week we would induction heat a can of Coca Cola. "Does it Blend" got millions of hits when it was popular. How many people would

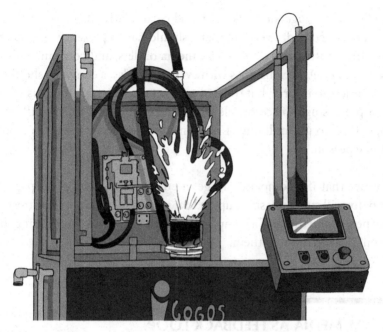

FIGURE 15.1
Induct This

have watched us blowing up shotgun shells and melting phones? It is impossible to say, but I can say that watching an induction heating machine heat metal is cool, even when it is just heating metal billets (Figure 15.1).

There was some tepid interest on the executive team but it did not go anywhere. Personally, I still think the idea was brilliant.

Had we done the YouTube videos, it would not have sold product, but if millions of people had watched the videos, some of them would have worked in industries related to induction heating, and getting our company logo in front of them could not possibly have hurt sales. At the very least it would have increased public knowledge about induction heating, while making our company look like a major player, and we could have interspersed into the videos neat information about the company, what it does, and what it is capable of. The actual blowing up of shotgun shells was the catch – the real purpose was to get a free commercial out there that both entertains and informs. We could have shown the videos in trade shows; the possibilities were endless.

Social media is huge for marketing, and particularly where younger audiences are concerned. Every company should have a presence on YouTube, LinkedIn, Twitter, and other social media outlets, and companies should take these outlets seriously. As with everything else, a company should use these outlets to inform, but the first goal is to be entertaining. It is far better to put a single piece of relevant information in front of millions of people than to put millions of relevant pieces of information in front of just one person.

Consider that if a company can get a customer to "like" their page, the company will suddenly show up on that person's feed every time the company posts something. If a company's posts are fun and entertaining, people will pay attention to them.

SOCIAL MEDIA AS FEEDBACK LOOP

As a company works with social media, don't just use it as a means of sending out entertaining marketing materials. Also use it to create the feedback loop between the customers and product engineering. Ask the customer their wants and needs. Ask the customer for ideas to improve products and services. If possible, make that feedback loop fun. Maybe offer a reward for any ideas that are utilized.

16

Waste

The first chapter of this book was dedicated to waste, as the "corrupt way to make money" relies on corruption, greed, cronyism, and a plethora of other things, all designed to take value *out* of the market.

An economy is nothing more than the everyday activities of people, living their everyday lives. As we pursue our needs and desires, we make economic decisions, both as producers, and consumers. We are producers over a very narrow, specific range of the economy, but we are consumers within a very wide range of industries. Whenever government activities interfere with our ability to pursue our own needs and desires, such as by taking our earnings and allocating them toward things we neither need, nor asked for, the government acts as an instrument of waste.

That's not to say that there is nothing the government does that adds value. There are, in fact, a number of things government does that add value for citizens. In fact, my next book will explore "Lean Governance." But overall, cronyism ("the corrupt way to make money") is arguably the biggest source of waste our country faces.

There are seven deadly wastes in lean: defects, overproduction, inventories, extra processing, motion, transport and handling, and waiting. Various authors add one or more of the following: underutilized human potential, unsafe/unergonomic work conditions, confusion about doing the right things at the right times, and failure to sustain lean practices. We've talked about most of these throughout the book (as any book on lean will do), but it is important to devote some time to describing waste directly.

The last four items are not really a part of the seven deadly wastes, and I'm not really sure they are "new" wastes, so much as additional things that can cause some of the seven deadly wastes. I'm including all four of them as I think they should be eliminated, whether we want to add them to the list, or not.

Lean is largely about *removing waste* and *adding value*. Some lean books focus more on the removing waste part. I probably focus more on the adding value part. The two are connected, however. Anything that does not add value is waste, and one cannot truly commit to removing waste without also focusing on value.

Companies should remove everything listed below as much as possible, everywhere they can, throughout the organization, whether in ways already listed in the book, or in other ways and other places that this book may not have covered directly.

A CHECKLIST OF SEVEN WASTES TO LOOK FOR AND MINIMIZE

Defects are self-explanatory. We discussed them in detail throughout the book, and particularly in the statistics and quality sections. When defects occur, companies are paying to make defective units they cannot sell.

Over production is simply making more than what customers want, or are willing to pay for.

Extra Processing is adding features customers do not want or cannot use, incurring costs for features that are not valued.

Inventories have been discussed at depth throughout this book. Extra, unsold inventory, comes at a cost to those who hold it.

Motion relates to having employees moving more than absolutely necessary. 5S is a big part of reducing motion, as are standardized processes that minimize the need to move. We talked about this in the standardization section. When this waste occurs, companies are paying people to move more than necessary to perform quality work.

Transportation and handling of goods is wasteful. It is of course impossible to get rid of all transportation and handling, but a company does want to minimize it by rearranging plants and offices so materials need to move as little as possible. Note that when moving inventory around, one is also transporting and handling goods. One-piece flow and balancing plants around bottlenecks can help to reduce transportation – both topics we have covered at length and particularly in the bottlenecks section. At the BMW plant in Spartanburg, SC, for example, some suppliers are next door, delivering parts directly to the assembly line via forklifts. No trucks, trains, or warehouses are needed for these parts.

Waiting for upstream processes was discussed in the bottleneck section. It is important to balance operations so that all operations run as close to takt time (without going over) as possible. We talked about this in Chapter 4.

Underutilized human potential was touched on in the Human Resource section, the automation section, and the layoffs section. Smart companies always want to develop their people and want to utilize everything their people can offer to their organization. A company should have succession plans as well. The right culture encourages employees to offer their process improvement ideas.

Unsafe or unergonomic work conditions are self-explanatory. We touched on this in the automation section. Injured workers cannot contribute.

Confusion leads not only to waiting, but also to mistakes – causing rework and defects. We discussed communication between departments and specific jobs at length throughout the book, ensuring that every employee in an organization knows exactly what output they need to produce to set the rest of the organization up for success. We discussed strategic planning in the strategic planning section and how it needs to filter all the way down to the bottom of the organization. As managers we need to look at what we communicate and, in addition, to be clear and concise.

Standardization in how and what is communicated can also clear up confusion, particularly where communications have a somewhat repetitive nature, such as in customer service.

Failure to sustain process improvements and Lean Culture. If companies spend time making improvements and then the employees don't keep using those improvements, companies are wasting the time and energy it took to improve. For a detailed solution to this, see *Sustain Your Gains*, by Michael McCarthy.

Conclusion

Lean Leadership Requires Systems Thinking

This book covered many topics in a relatively short space. The goal has not been to teach how to run a marketing department, how to perform strategic planning, or how to do any of the other specific items covered, so much as to make the reader think differently about how all of the items within a business work together as a system. The goal is to teach how to look at employees, companies, and missions, in terms of how they connect to one another, and in terms of how they relate to the marketplace and society at large.

Everyone in an organization, from the CEO down, exists for a reason, and that is to create the output needed by others. Every manager must constantly align internal customers with internal suppliers, improving the output suppliers produce, to better meet the needs of internal customers. The manager has customers: their employees. Managers need to provide employees what employees need to do their jobs.

Each employee, each process, and each department exists, not as a solitary unit, but as a subsystem within larger systems. Just as an old clock can only perform its mission if every gear is the correct size, with the correct number of teeth, correctly placed and correctly tuned to all of the other gears in the clock, so too a company can only perform if all of its pieces fit. Some old clocks have thousands of gears, and a clock can only be accurate if every one of them is doing exactly what it is supposed to do, exactly when it is supposed to do it. Every part of an organization must be constantly adjusted, to best meet the needs of larger (and smaller) systems and subsystems.

A WASTED PAYCHECK?

When I was a Specialist in the Army, on the verge of being promoted to Sergeant, I was told that being a Sergeant does not necessarily make someone a Non-Commissioned Officer (NCO). Rather, an NCO is someone people willingly follow, even into combat. People follow NCOs when they trust and respect them, when they feel the NCO has their interests (as well as their mission) at heart, and when the NCO's actions speak with clarity of purpose and integrity of intent. An NCO who does not inspire others is "just a sergeant." Real NCO's "walk the walk."

Every manager within an organization, and particularly the CEO, needs to "walk the walk." A manager who fails to lead by example is not really a manager at all, but is, rather, a wasted pay check.

Most CEOs and business owners understand their companies. Hopefully, this book can help them to also understand how their organizations serve customers in the larger society. I am not suggesting some altruistic "shareholders over stockholders" nonsense, but I do suggest that a company can only be successful if it adds value for customers. I am suggesting that the amount of profit earned is directly related to the amount of value provided to the customer. The best thing a company can do for its stockholders is to look at profit as a necessary byproduct of the value the company provides to customers. Conversely, if customers, for whatever reason, do not want what a company produces, then no value is created, profit becomes impossible, and the company vanishes, like Radio Shack or MySpace.com.

THE WAY FORWARD IS TO INNOVATE

Value and niche go hand in hand, and the companies that add the most value, within each niche, profit most. A business person has to understand their market, as well as their competitors, and has to position their company where they can add more value than can anyone else. Only one company can be the high cost, quality leader. Only one company can be the cheapest alternative. If a company can lead in quality as well as cost, that's great, but if a company cannot lead in everything, pick a niche and get out in front.

Most entrepreneurial companies eventually need to reinvent themselves. Innovative ideas do not stay innovative forever (flip phones, anyone?), and the falling profits of maturing industries cause large players to squeeze-out smaller competitors. The way forward is to innovate, creating new opportunities, in new market segments, with new techniques, and new technologies. Kodak actually invented digital photography, but did not develop that market segment. Now Kodak is a fraction of its former size.

In the meantime, process innovation allows current operations to continue more efficiently, by squeezing waste out of what is already done. Product and process innovation are both important, and which is more important changes over time.

Standardization and improvement methodologies reduce waste, funding new market segments, and/or entirely new markets. This sort of innovation is not easy, but if a company is focused, and if it is willing to change existing cultural norms, this kind of innovation becomes not only possible, but a part of a company's DNA. The 3M Company has a goal that 20% of its sales will come from products that did not exist five years ago. Innovation is in 3M's DNA.

Company culture is either a company's greatest source of competitive advantage, or the greatest source of disadvantage. If an executive team builds the right culture, then their company will do well. If an executive team is fighting amongst itself (with members pandering for political favor), then they are not taking care of the business, and the business will suffer.

EMPLOYEES ARE THE SOURCE OF INNOVATION

There is nothing healthier than the firing of bad employees. Layoffs, on the other hand, kill culture. Nobody wants to work themselves out of a job, so if a company wants employees to think about what they do, and to constantly *improve* upon what they do, then layoffs are a no-go. Employees may decide to leave on their own, they may retire, or the company may move them to different positions (where they can add more value), but employees must feel secure in their employment if they are to remain loyal, and help the company improve.

While a company should never lay-off permanent employees, laying off temps is fine. All companies should have a pool of temps during the good times. It can reduce them when necessary.

Some of the knowledge "where the rubber meets the road" is mundane, compared to the specialized knowledge at the top of an organization, but that mundane knowledge about how processes actually work is far more valuable, in the aggregate, than is the specialized knowledge at the top of the organization. Improvement ideas are valuable no matter where they come from.

CUSTOMERS: FIRST, LAST AND ALWAYS

The people within a company know their own products, but *customers* know what they *want* from those products. Customers know what improvements they would like to see, and more importantly, what improvements they would be willing to pay for. If a company's engineers are leading the charge on design changes, rather than customers leading that charge (with marketing acting as a feedback loop), then that company is not going to make the improvements customers want. Remember Kodak.

The first rule in marketing is to entertain, so make sure marketing materials are fun. If the people who make marketing materials don't want to read them, neither will customers.

Engage consumers on social media, and make that engagement fun.

IF YOU DON'T MEASURE IT, YOU CAN'T IMPROVE IT

Managers often ignore statistics. Some even disparage statistics. Understand that if a company does not measure what is going on within it, then there is no way to know whether a change is making things better, or worse. Only by measuring critical metrics throughout the organization, and understanding the difference between common cause and special cause variation, can companies improve. Failure to measure is an abdication of management.

Think sports teams. A team's win/loss record is equivalent to market share. Stats like RBI, yards passing, etc., are the sports equivalent to statistical process control measurements. Winning coaches pay attention to these stats. Improving these stats is the path to winning. For more examples, read *Moneyball*, by Michael Lewis.

MAKE VALUE, NOT REGULATIONS

I am not going to lie and say that in our current cronyist economy, people cannot make money by bribing government to extort money from the public. People absolutely do that, and those who do it well often make a lot of money. Unless one is a really big player, however, control over government is an illusion, and the political winds are both fickle and unforgiving. The crony game is like a casino: eventually everything goes back to the house. The "house" is the government.

Don't use government to force your customers to do business with you. Make your company the one customers *want* to do business with, not the one customers *have* to do business with because of government regulations. Think CFL light bulbs, mandated by the government. The mercury in the bulbs created a health risk if the bulb was broken. Customers *want* to do business with a company that gives them the most value for their money. Cree introduced retail LED light bulbs that are safe, use less energy, and last longer. People *wanted* to buy their products. *Be that company.*

Value, not profit, is the lifeblood of business. If a company becomes truly value-adding, it will grow to be the dominant business in its industry. The profits will follow. Think Amazon.

I opened this book with a story about a company I once worked for, that failed to compete successfully within it's chosen market. I'll close by inviting the reader to reach out and share any success stories that were inspired by reading this book. You may send your success stories to www.thewayforwardbook.com.

Glossary

5S A workplace organization method that uses a list of five words: "Sort," "Set In order," "Shine," "Standardize," and "Sustain." The list describes how to organize a work space for efficiency and effectiveness by identifying and storing the items used, maintaining the area and items, and sustaining the new order. The decision-making process usually comes from a dialogue about standardization, which builds understanding among employees of how they should do the work.

Activity-Based Costing A costing method that identifies activities in an organization and assigns the cost of each activity to all products and services according to the actual consumption by each. This model assigns more indirect costs into direct costs compared to conventional costing. Cima defines abc as an approach to the costing and monitoring of activities which involves tracing resource consumption and costing final outputs.

Alignment The proper adjustment of the components of an electronic circuit, machine, etc., for coordinated functioning. Also used to describe strategies at each level of the company that support one another.

Automation The use of largely automatic equipment in a system of manufacturing or other production process.

Batch Processing The performing of an industrial process on material in batches of a limited quantity or number.

Bottleneck A narrow section of road or a junction that impedes traffic flow. In lean parlance, the process, or processes, that sets the pace of an organization.

Cash-Cow A business, investment, or product that provides a steady income or profit.

Common Cause Variation Fluctuation caused by unknown factors resulting in a steady but random distribution of output around the average of the data. It is a measure of the process potential, or how well the process can perform when special cause variation removed.

Competitive Advantage A condition or circumstance that puts a company in a favorable or superior business position.

Constraints A limitation or restriction. In lean parlance, the belief that bottlenecks constrain the output of organizations.

Control Chart Also known as Shewhart charts (after Walter A. Shewhart) or process-behavior charts, are a statistical process control tool used to determine if a manufacturing or business process is in a state of control.

Control Limits Also known as natural process limits, are horizontal lines drawn on a statistical process control chart, usually at a distance of ±3 standard deviations of the plotted statistic from the statistic's mean.

Critical Measurements Critical product measurements (cpk) **Statistical measurements of the process capability** in terms of its design specifications (limits) and performance (variability).

Cronyism An economic system characterized by close, mutually advantageous relationships between business leaders and government officials.

Current State A present set of circumstances. The way a process is currently performed.

Cycle Times The average time between the start of production of one unit and the start of production of the next unit.

Defects   A shortcoming, imperfection, or lack.

Defensive Tasks   Tasks performed to make processes more difficult, or more cumbersome, than necessary.

Economies of Scale   The cost advantages that enterprises obtain due to their scale of operation (typically measured by amount of output produced), with cost per unit of output decreasing with increasing scale. At the basis of economies of scale there may be technical, statistical, organizational, or related factors to the degree of market control.

Efficiencies of Build   The cost advantages that enterprises obtain by removing as much waste as possible from each individual build of a finished good or service.

Empowerment   Authority or power given to someone to do something.

ERP System   A suite of integrated applications—that an organization can use to collect, store, manage, and interpret data from many business activities.

Fiefdom   The part of a business a person controls, when used for personal or political purposes, rather than for the business as a whole.

Finished Goods   Goods that have completed the manufacturing process but have not yet been sold or distributed to the end user.

Five Why Analysis   A system used to determine the root cause of a problem. A root cause is one that goes all the way back to the beginning of how the problem started in the first place.

Fixed Costs   A cost that does not change with an increase or decrease in the amount of goods or services produced or sold.

Flow Chart   A diagram of the sequence of movements or actions of people or things involved in a complex system or activity.

Forester's Whip   A distribution channel phenomenon in which forecasts yield supply chain inefficiencies. It refers to increasing swings in inventory in response to shifts in customer demand as one moves further up the supply chain.

Free Market   An economic system in which prices are determined by unrestricted competition between privately owned businesses.

Future State   A future set of circumstances. The way a process will be performed after changes are standardized.

Gemba   The place where things are built in manufacturing, or other business operations.

Human Resources   The personnel of a business or organization, especially when regarded as a significant asset. The department of a business or organization that deals with the hiring, administration, and training of personnel.

Hypothesis   A supposition or proposed explanation made on the basis of limited evidence as a starting point for further investigation.

Ideal State   A theoretical "perfect way" to perform a process.

Internal Efficiencies   The efficiencies of an internal system or process, without regard for how that process affects other, larger systems and processes.

Inventory   A complete list of items such as property, goods in stock, or the contents of a building.

Inventory Management System   The combination of technology (hardware and software) and processes and procedures that oversee the monitoring and maintenance of stocked products, whether those products are company assets, raw materials, and supplies, or finished products ready to be sent to vendors or end consumers.

Kaizen A Japanese business philosophy of continuous improvement of working practices, personal efficiency, etc.

Kaizen Event (or rapid improvement event) Dedicating a team of people from 2 to 5 days to study a process and test improvements to that process. End result: an improved process that becomes the new standard work.

Labor Productive activity, especially for the sake of economic gain, and the people who perform this activity.

Lead Times The time between the initiation and completion of a production process.

Lean Manufacturing An assembly-line methodology developed originally for Toyota and the manufacturing of automobiles. It is also known as the Toyota Production System or just-in-time production. Lean production principles are also referred to as lean management or lean thinking.

Limits of Demand The concept that demand for a product will at some point peak, and perhaps decline.

Manual Process Processes performed through manual labor.

Market Segment A group of people who share one or more common characteristics, lumped together for marketing purposes.

Market Share The portion of a market controlled by a particular company or product.

Marketing The business process of creating relationships with and satisfying customers through a value exchange.

Mass Manufacturing A manufacturing process or technique that began during the industrial revolution based on reducing per-part costs through the production of more parts.

Maturing Markets Markets where equilibrium exists and there is a lack of change or innovation.

Operations A piece of organized and concerted activity involving a number of people.

Out of Control A process with multiple points occurring more than three sigma from the mean.

Permatemps Temporary workers kept on a permanent basis.

PERT A method of analyzing the tasks involved in completing a given project, especially the time needed to complete each task, and to identify the minimum time needed to complete the total project.

Process Charts A visual representation of the sequence of steps and decisions needed to perform a process.

Process Improvement A systematic approach to closing of process or system performance gaps through streamlining and cycle time reduction, and identification and elimination of causes of below specifications quality, process variation, and non-value-adding activities.

Process Innovation The implementation of a new or significantly improved production or delivery method.

Processing Time The period required to complete one cycle of an operation; or to complete a function, job, or task from start to finish.

Product Engineers A Mechanical Engineer who specializes in designing products and their corresponding manufacturing processes.

Product Innovation The development and market introduction of a new, redesigned, or substantially improved good or service.

Profit Margin The amount by which revenue from sales exceeds costs in a business.

Profit Sharing A system in which the people who work for a company receive a direct share of the profits.

Profitability The degree to which a business or activity yields profit or financial gain.

Qs9000 A quality standard developed by a joint effort of the "Big Three" American automakers, General Motors, Chrysler, and Ford. It was introduced to the industry in 1994. It has been adopted by several heavy truck manufacturers in the U.S. as well.

Quality The standard of something as measured against other things of a similar kind; the degree of excellence of something. Now defined in Lean as meeting customer requirements.

Quality Output Quality, as defined by one's customers.

Question Mark Quadrant A new product that has not yet proven itself in the market.

Rapid Changeover The ability to change a machine from making one kind of part, to another, quickly – ideally in the time it takes to make one part.

Raw Materials The basic material from which a product is made.

Regression to Mean The phenomenon that arises if a random variable is extreme on its first measurement but closer to the mean or average on its second measurement and if it is extreme on its second measurement but closer to the average on its first.

Root-Cause Analysis A method of problem-solving used for identifying the root causes of faults or problems.

SIPOC A tool that summarizes the inputs and outputs of one or more processes in table form. The acronym SIPOC stands for suppliers, inputs, process, outputs, and customers.

Six Sigma   A set of techniques and tools for process improvement. It was introduced by American engineer Bill Smith while working at Motorola in 1980. Jack Welch made it central to his business strategy at General Electric in 1995. A Six Sigma process is one in which 99.99966% of all opportunities to produce some feature of a part are statistically expected to be free of defects.

Special Cause Variation   Variation in a process which is sporadic and non-random.

Special Interests   A person or group seeking to influence legislative or government policy to further often narrowly defined interests.

Standardization   The process of making something conform to a standard.

Statistics Based Management   A style of management that uses statistics, and statistical analysis, to find and solve problems, as well as to make systemic improvements to processes.

Strategic Alliances   Agreements among firms in which each commits resources to achieve a common set of objectives

Supply Chain   The active management of supply chain activities to maximize customer value and achieve a sustainable competitive advantage.

Systemization   The act of creating a new system. The primary benefit of creating a system is that you can examine the process and make improvements.

Systems Theory   The interdisciplinary study of systems. A system is a cohesive conglomeration of interrelated and interdependent parts which can be natural or human-made. Every system is bounded by space and time, influenced by its environment, defined by its structure and purpose, and expressed through its functioning. A system may be more than the sum of its parts if it expresses synergy or emergent behavior.

Systems Thinking A holistic approach to analysis that focuses on the way that a system's constituent parts interrelate and how systems work over time and within the context of larger systems. The systems thinking approach contrasts with traditional analysis, which studies systems by breaking them down into their separate elements.

Tactical Proficiency The ability to apply a job within a practical business environment.

Takt Time The "pace" of production. Calculated as the available production time divided by the average number of units ordered by the customer. If you are meeting takt time you are making enough to fulfill customer orders.

Tampering with the Process Responses that treat common-cause variation as special-cause variation.

Technical Proficiency The ability to perform a job within technical standards.

Temporary Workers Workers hired through a temporary agency, generally to be used on a temporary basis.

Theory of Constraints A management paradigm that views any manageable system as being limited in achieving goals by a very small number of constraints. There is always at least one constraint, and TOC uses a focusing process to identify the constraint and restructure the rest of the organization around it.

Throughput The amount of material or items passing through a system or process.

Toyota Production System The production control system established by Toyota, based on many years of continuous improvements, with the objective of making the vehicles ordered by customers in the quickest and most efficient way, in order to deliver the vehicles as swiftly as possible.

Truth in Advertising Laws designed to ensure that advertising is honest and truthful.

Turns The number of times inventory is turned-over (sold) in a process, or a retail space.

Usage Point The point (measured in time) where half of a given product will have become unserviceable.

Value The importance, worth, or usefulness of something. What a customer will pay for.

Value Stream Map A lean-management method for analyzing the current state and designing a future state for the series of events that take a product or service from the beginning of the specific process until it reaches the customer.

Value-Adding Activities Any activities that add value to the customer and meet the three criteria for a Value-Adding Activity. The three criteria for a Value-Adding Activity are: The step transforms the item toward completion. The step is done right the first time (not a rework step) The customer wants (or would pay) for the step to be done.

Variable Costs A cost that varies with the level of output.

Wait Times The amount of time a job is sitting ideal before the order is processed or the machine is setup.

Waste An act or instance of using or expending something carelessly, extravagantly, or to no purpose. In Lean, using more than is necessary.

INDEX

Page numbers in *italic* indicate figures. Page numbers in n indicate notes.

Printed in the United States
by Baker & Taylor Publisher Services